Sweater RENEWAL

Sweater RENEWAL

FELTING KNITS INTO NEW SWEATERS AND ACCESSORIES

Sharon Franco Rothschild

PHOTOGRAPHY BY ANTHONY-MASTERSON

POTTER
CRAFT

NEW YORK

The author and publisher would like to thank the Craft Yarn Council of America for providing the yarn weight standards and accompanying icons used in this book. For more information, please visit www.YarnStandards.com.

Published in the United States by Potter Craft, an imprint of the Crown Publishing Group, a division of Random House, Inc., New York.
www.crownpublishing.com
www.pottercraft.com

POTTER CRAFT and colophon is a registered trademark of Random House, Inc.

Library of Congress Cataloging-in-Publication Data

Rothschild, Sharon Franco.
Sweater renewal : felting knits into new sweaters and accessories / Sharon Franco Rothschild.— 1st ed.
p. cm.
Includes index.
ISBN-13: 978-0-307-39629-7
1. Felt work. 2. Felting. I. Title.
TT849.5.R67 2008
746'.0463—dc22   2008003354

ISBN 978-0-307-39629-7

Printed in China

Contributors:
Technical editing by Sylvia Carroll
Styling and make-up by Mordechai Alvow
Template illustrations by Janine Lecour
Project illustrations by Sharon Franco Rothschild
Photography by Anthony-Masterson Photographers, Atlanta
Design by Chalkley Calderwood

10 9 8 7 6 5 4 3 2 1

First Edition

This book is dedicated to my late father, David M. Franco,
who felted his first sweater (quite by accident) many years ago,
never knowing that one day it would lead me into the fascinating
world of sweaters and, ultimately, this book.

CONTENTS

INTRODUCTION

I am, and always will be, a self-confessed sweater junkie. Whether I am designing, knitting, buying, felting, cutting, or wearing sweaters, I can never get enough of them. Sweaters provide comfort, warmth, and a certain sense of style.

We all have our favorites—some that make us feel fabulously stylish, some that make us feel incredibly comfortable, and those that offer a coziness and warmth that no other piece of clothing can compete with. As we collect and add sweaters to our wardrobes year after year, memories also attach themselves to each piece.

I will forever remember one of my all-time favorite sweaters, and its quick demise. I was sixteen years old, and the sweater (I can remember it like it was yesterday) was a pink mohair cardigan, the exact color of cotton candy. When I wore this sweater, I felt transformed. I felt grown up, stylish, even beautiful. But one of my father's first attempts to do the laundry for our family ended in disaster for this cherished piece of clothing. After some washing-machine agitation (in hot water, no less), my beautiful sweater shrank down to one-third its original size and was suddenly and completely unwearable. But my love affair with this sweater was not yet over. I kept it in my top dresser drawer, and every time I opened that drawer, I would look at my pink sweater and remember instantly how good it had made me feel. It was years before I could actually part with it. How I wish now that I had made something else out of it, something that I could have continued to use in my daily life, to remind me of my dad and the wonderful feeling that sweater had given me. It could have been a pillow, a purse, or any one of the twenty-five projects featured in this book.

Fortunately, I have discovered that damaged sweaters, old sweaters, out-of-style sweaters, and sweaters that once belonged to a loved one can have a second life. The projects in *Sweater Renewal* are for crafters of all skill levels, from beginners to the more experienced. Techniques include felting, appliqué, crochet, knitting, sewing, and embroidery, and each is accompanied by easy-to-follow, step-by-step directions. You don't even need to know how to knit or crochet, but if you do, you can incorporate these techniques into your projects. For the dedicated knitters out there, I have included a few projects to knit first, then wash and felt later. Most of the projects in the book can be finished in less than a day; some in a few hours. You can follow the patterns exactly, or be inspired by what you see here and create your own individual works of art. There are detailed instructions on how to felt using a washing machine or by hand, if you choose.

Now is the time to go through your attic, basement, and even your closets to look for good candidates. You can recapture old memories and help save the planet by using old blankets, men's sweaters, women's sweaters, children's sweaters, and even hand-knitted sweater pieces (I think almost every knitter has a stash of those buried somewhere). The only requirement is that they be made out of wool. So clean out your closets, start your washing machines, sharpen your scissors, and get ready to redesign, recycle, and renew your wool sweaters. Instant gratification is just a few steps away!

DON'T THROW OUT OLD WOOL SWEATERS—GIVE THEM A NEW LIFE BY FELTING AND STITCHING THEM INTO THE PROJECTS IN THIS BOOK.

THE HISTORY OF FELTING

Attila the Hun did it. Genghis Khan did it. Now you can do it, too! These infamous historical figures and their tribes were known as the "makers of felted tents," and were among the first to discover the process of felting.

Wool, the protein fiber that comes from sheep, is one of the most widely used and completely renewable resources in the world. For thousands of years, humans have sheared sheep for their fleece, which, when put through a process that combines heat, moisture, and agitation, turns into a fabric called felt. Felting is the earliest form of textile processing known to humans, and it has played an important role in human survival throughout history.

The felting process can be traced back to before the first century, when Asian nomadic tribes learned to survive freezing temperatures and extreme conditions by using their herds of sheep and goats to provide shelter and clothing. These tribes were among the first to domesticate the horse, and they would take pieces of sheared fleece, tuck them underneath a horse's saddle, and ride horseback for days. The moisture and body heat from the horse, combined with the agitation from the saddle, created pieces of felt from the fleece. This felt would then be used to make tents, blankets, and clothing. It wasn't until thousands of years later that raw fleece was used to spin yarn, and weaving and knitting were invented.

There are two different types of felting. The first, and oldest, type of felt is the result of exposing raw fleece to heat, moisture, and agitation in order to create a fabriclike material. The second type, which is described in this book, occurs when heat, moisture, and agitation are applied to an already knitted garment or blanket. This type of felting is sometimes referred to as *fulling*, which is basically the same as felting, but easier and less time-consuming than the first method (since your washing machine does all the work). The term *fulling* comes from the Latin word *fullare*, which means "to walk on or trample." This process emphasizes the agitation that is required to make the fiber scales lock together.

FELTABLE FIBERS

Sheep are not the only animals that produce feltable fiber. Goats, llamas, and rabbits also give us the gift that keeps on giving. Each of these animals provides a fiber that can be spun into yarn and used to knit garments. These knitted garments can then be felted, using the instructions in this book.

Cashmere, which comes from goats, is one of the most luxurious fibers around. Goats that graze in cold climates and high altitudes produce the best quality cashmere. Cashmere sweaters felt beautifully. They tend to be more expensive than wool sweaters, of course, but you can find them in vintage and thrift shops for very reasonable prices.

Alpaca is known as the "poor man's cashmere," but it is by no means a cheap fiber. Alpaca comes from alpacas, which are native to South America, but more and more alpaca farms are popping up all over the United States due to the increasing popularity of and demand for the fiber, as well as the animals themselves. As the number of alpacas in our country increases, their fiber becomes more abundant and readily available. Alpaca sweaters also felt beautifully.

Lamb's wool has a much softer and finer texture than wool that comes from fully grown sheep. Sweaters made from lamb's wool tend to be lighter and softer than those made of regular wool, especially when made from the underlying fleece of the lamb.

Angora, which comes from rabbits, is the furriest, fluffiest fiber of them all. Unlike other fiber-producing animals, rabbits are not sheared; they're brushed. And because they shed very easily, this makes for a much less involved collection process. French Angora bunnies are much fluffier and produce more hair than their American cousins. When angora is spun into yarn, knitted, and then felted, it may take on the appearance of fur.

Mohair is a silky, long-hair fiber that comes from the angora goat (not to be confused with the angora rabbit). This fiber has a high luster and sheen to it and is used in combination with other fibers to enhance the overall look of a finished product. Mohair accepts dyes extremely well, and you will find mohair sweaters available in very bright and vibrant colors. It is also a good fiber for felting.

WOOL RULES

Rule #1. Sweaters must be at least 85 percent wool, cashmere, alpaca, lamb's wool, or angora.
Always be sure to check the labels of sweaters before you use them. If you choose a woolen that contains a mix of more than 15 percent cotton, acrylic, or other synthetic fibers, that may prevent the wool from felting. One hundred percent of any of these fibers is best, but anything at 85 percent or above will definitely work. Anything less than that may or may not work—and the only way to know for sure is to felt the sweater and see what happens.

Rule #2. Heat + Moisture + Agitation = Felting.
Just remember: The higher the heat, the longer the washing, the more the agitation, the smaller and thicker your piece will get. It's all about the shrinkage—and timing is everything! You might want to experiment by cutting a sweater into four separate pieces. Try washing the first piece on a very short, gentle cycle, in warm water. Wash the second piece for a few minutes longer, in warmer water. Continue to increase the length and type of wash cycle and the water temperature, with the fourth piece being washed at the longest cycle and in the hottest water. Generally, you can expect anywhere from a 20-30 percent shrinkage, although there will always be exceptions.

Rule #3. Not all sweaters are the same.
Wool will not always shrink or felt the same way. You cannot expect the exact same outcome for every sweater you felt. As you become more experienced with the process, you will become more knowledgeable about the possibilities depending on yarn, fiber, and pattern used. Keep a notebook, and write down the details of each sweater that you wash and what the outcome was. This will serve as valuable information each time you try to felt a different sweater.

FELTING METHODS

There are three methods for felting sweaters: in your washing machine, by hand in your sink or tub, or at your local dry cleaner. The washing-machine method is the easiest and fastest way to felt, especially if you are washing a whole sweater or blanket. If you are doing a small piece, such as a sock, a hat, or a cut piece of a sweater, you may find the hand-washing method easier. If you do not want to deal with the actual washing and felting yourself, your local dry cleaner is a good alternative.

Washing-Machine Felting
There are two types of washing machines—top loaders and front loaders. Top loaders open at the top of the machine, and you put your clothes in a basketlike

container that has a cylinder in the middle. Top loaders work best for sweater felting for two reasons. The first is that you can open the top at any time during the wash cycle and check your felting. The second is that the cylinder in the middle provides a lot of agitation, so your sweater will felt very quickly, often in one cycle.

Front loaders have a door that opens in the front of the machine, and they provide a much larger, more open space than a top loader. Once the wash cycle begins, the door automatically locks and cannot be opened until the cycle is finished. Because there is no spin basket in the front loader, there is less agitation. So with front loaders, I suggest that you begin any felting project using a very short cycle (hand-wash is best) and know that you may need to go through a few cycles before your sweater will felt the way you want it to.

How to Felt Using the Washing Machine

- Place your item in a pillowcase. This will protect your piece and provide more friction (which is a good thing).
- Select a very short cycle to begin. The hand-wash cycle is always a safe bet.
- Set the water temperature to WARM.
- Add about ¼ cup (60ml) of Ivory liquid soap, or any dishwashing liquid with a low pH balance.
- Select the shortest spin cycle and the gentlest wash cycle. Spinning the item for too long can distort the shape of the piece, but it needs to spin a little so all the water comes out.
- Place the pillowcase with your item inside in the washing machine. Start your washing machine. Do not felt more than one piece at a time. After each cycle, take your piece out of the pillowcase and check to see if you need to wash it again.
- When you have achieved the desired results, put your item in the dryer (still in the pillowcase). Run the dryer on a very low- or no-heat setting until the item is dry. Now you are ready to begin one of the projects in the book. Get out your scissors and start cutting!

Felting by Hand

This process requires some elbow grease—and for your hands to be submerged in water for a while. Make sure you have a pair of rubber gloves to wear so your hands don't get waterlogged! The rubber also provides good friction for felting. If you're felting in your bathtub, use a rubber plunger—it works great!

How to Felt by Hand

- Fill the sink (use the tub if you're felting a large item) with warm water. Add a few tablespoons of Ivory liquid soap, or any dishwashing liquid with a low pH balance.
- Using your hands, agitate and rub the soapy piece together with moderate force. You will begin to notice the fiber becoming softer and fuzzier. Continue until you are unable to see the stitches clearly, which means that the fiber is felting. This process is a lot slower than using a machine, but it does work well when a washing machine is not available (and it gives your arms a great workout at the same time)!
- When you are satisfied with the results, squeeze out the water from your woolen item, roll it up in a towel, and squeeze out all excess water.
- Place your felted piece in a pillowcase and put it in the dryer. Run the dryer on a very low- or no-heat setting until the item is dry. If you don't have access to a dryer, hang your felted piece on a clothesline to dry.

Dry Cleaners

If in doubt, or if you are just not ready to take the plunge, there is always your local dry cleaner. These establishments have commercial washers and dryers, and most are willing to work with you if you explain your desired outcome. Be very specific about sizing and the amount of shrinkage you desire. They will probably make you sign a waiver, since normally they are paid *not* to shrink sweaters.

FELTING FACTORS

Because felting will never be an exact science, the amount of shrinkage in each individual garment will vary depending on these factors: the amount of time in the washer, the temperature of the water, the degree of agitation, and the makeup of the fiber. Even subtle things, such as the dye color of the yarn, can affect the way a sweater shrinks. There is no precise formula to follow. Practice and patience will almost make perfect. The more you felt, the more you will know about felting. It will feel like a big experiment, and your laundry room will feel like a laboratory—where you will blend your art and science skills to create your own individual masterpiece!

ALL ABOUT COLOR

I love color! Bold, bright, and sometimes shocking, it can be a wonderful way to express ourselves. My world of color first began in college, during my first color theory class. Our assignment was to re-create an entire color wheel, showing the complete range and spectrum of color. Using tubes of paint in the primary colors, red, yellow, and blue, we had to measure and mix these colors together (with black and white paint) to create dozens of colors. It was an exercise in training our eyes to see colors in a different way, and it opened up a world of color and endless possibilities for me! You should experiment with using many different color combinations. The same project, done in another color, will look completely different. So be bold, take chances, and combine your colors in unexpected ways. You'll be amazed at what a difference color can make!

COZY DRAGONFLY NEEDLE HOLDER, PAGE 16

CHAPTER 1. SHORT, SWEET & SIMPLE:
BEGINNING PROJECTS

The six projects in this first chapter are small in size and can be completed in just a few hours. This is a good place to start if you are a beginning felter; the projects only call for working with pieces of sweaters, so the sizing and amount of shrinkage are not that important. Play around with different sweaters and really push the limits of how much you can felt something. If the garment shrinks too much, you will still be able to find a use for it with the projects in this chapter. If you'd like to felt sweaters that are damaged or stained or you want to use pieces of hand-knitting that were never finished, this is the chapter for you. Finally, be sure to save all the leftover pieces of felt you create—these scraps are perfect for the appliquéd shapes that are featured later in the book.

COZY DRAGONFLY NEEDLE HOLDER

Knitting needles and socks have two things in common: They come in matching pairs, and one of them is always disappearing. I have a drawer where I keep all my singular socks. I can't seem to throw them out; I keep hoping that, one day, their opposite number will magically reappear. These errant socks almost never do. I also used to have a drawer full of my unmatched knitting needles, that is, until I designed this cozy needle holder. Now all my pairs of needles are tucked happily into their own individual covers, arranged in a basket in the den. They're so bright and colorful that it's almost like looking at fresh flowers every day. The materials listed here are for a turquoise holder, but feel free to experiment with different color combinations to fill your own colorful basket. This project is a simple one, and in no time at all, your needles can be organized and displayed beautifully.

Finished Measurements

To fit 10" (25.5cm) needles:
1" (2.5cm) w x 9" (22.8cm) h

To fit 14" (35.5cm) needles:
1" (2.5cm) w x 12" (30.5cm) h

Materials

Turquoise sweater made of mostly feltable fibers (see pages 10-11), at least 4½" x 17¼" (11.4cm x 44cm)

 1 skein each Rowan Classic Cashsoft 4-ply yarn, 57% extra fine merino, 33% microfibre, 10% cashmere, 1.75 oz (50g), 197 yd (180m), in dark red and light brown (light brown for optional crochet flower)

4 skeins of size 25 embroidery floss in dark red, deep pink, purple, and orange

Approximately 36 2mm seed beads in assorted colors

Eight 4mm seed beads, two each in orange, black, red, and lime green

Two 8mm fuchsia-colored jingle bells

Small box of straight pins

DMC #5 embroidery needle

Beadalon big eye beading needle 2 (5.7cm)

Tapestry needle

Size G-6 (4mm) crochet hook (optional)

Techniques

Washing and felting (pages 11-12)

Embroidery: Lazy daisy stitch (page 117), running stitch (page 117)

Crochet (optional): Slip stitch (page 118), chain stitch (page 118), single crochet (page 118)

FELT THE SWEATER

1. Follow the general instructions for washing and felting the sweater on pages 10–11.

CUT OUT THE HOLDER & EMBROIDER THE DRAGONFLIES

cut
felted sweater

1 piece

2. Cut out a rectangle from the felted sweater in the size desired. For 14" (35.5cm) needles, cut the rectangle 3" x 12" (7.5cm x 30.5cm). For 10" (25cm) needles, cut the rectangle 3" x 9" (7.5cm x 23cm).

3. Using the embroidery floss and lazy daisy stitch, make four long wings (two on each side) and two short wings (one on each side) for each dragonfly. Each of the four dragonflies has different colored wings—see photo. Start about 2" (5cm) below the top edging and place a set of dragonfly wings every 2" (5cm) for the length of your holder (see photo). Embroider the wings so that the dragonflies face an upward diagonal angle in alternating directions (first toward the left, then toward the right, etc.).

4. To make each dragonfly body, place six 2mm seed beads of the same color on the thread and sew them to the holder lengthwise across the middle of the dragonfly's wings. For each set of eyes, sew two 4mm seed beads of the same color at the top front of the dragonfly's body.

ASSEMBLE & FINISH

5. Fold the holder lengthwise with wrong sides facing and pin together. Using a ½" (13mm) seam allowance and a machine- or hand-running stitch, sew down the length and across one end. Trim the excess seam allowance to eliminate bulk. Turn the holder right side out.

6. Turn under the top edge and machine-stitch or hand-sew around the edge for added security.

7. Using dark-red yarn and the tapestry needle, finish with blanket stitches around the top edge.

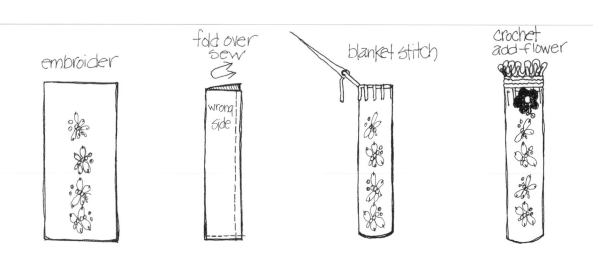

embroider

fold over
sew

wrong
side

blanket stitch

crochet
add flower

CROCHET TOP (OPTIONAL)

8. Using a crochet hook, join the yarn to the blanket stitch with a slip stitch. Begin making single crochet stitches attached to the blanket stitches all around the holder. When you get back to the beginning, single crochet in each single crochet. Continue in a spiral manner for approximately 1" (2.5cm). On the next round, chain 6 or 7 between each single crochet to create a ruffled edge. Tie off the yarn and weave in the end.

MAKE DANGLES

9. At the center front top of the holder, take the needle with the yarn from the inside to the outside, leaving a 2" (5cm) tail on the inside. Thread approximately six assorted 2mm beads on the yarn. Thread the yarn through the loop of a jingle bell, and then back up through the beads. Take the needle to the inside, pulling the beads up to the holder, then back to the outside right beside the first dangle of beads. Repeat for a second dangle. Take the yarn to the inside again and tie the yarn tails together in a secure knot. Clip the excess yarn.

CROCHET FLOWER (OPTIONAL)

10. With the light-brown yarn, crochet a five-petal flower (page 119). Thread the two tail ends of yarn from the flower through the holder from the outside to the inside at the top of the dangles, as shown in the photograph. Tie the two tails together in a secure knot to attach the flower to the holder.

BEE BOOKMARK

Never dog-ear the corner of a book page again! With this whimsical bookmark you can add a sense of style to whatever you are reading. Make several of them to keep on hand, and every time you give someone a book, be sure to include one of these bookmarks to personalize your gift.

Finished Measurements

1¾" (7cm) w x 6⅛" (15.5cm) h

Materials

Apple-green sweater made of mostly feltable fibers (see pages 10–11), at least 5" x 9" (12.5cm x 23cm)

¾" x 6" (2cm x 15cm) piece of cardboard

1 skein size 25 aqua embroidery floss

Approximately 40 2mm seed beads in red

Thirteen 2mm seed beads in pink

Beading wire, at least 27" long

Small box of straight pins

DMC embroidery needle #5

Sewing needle and clear thread

Techniques

Washing and felting (pages 11–12)

Embroidery: Blanket stitch (page 116)

FELT THE SWEATER

1. Follow the general instructions for washing and felting the sweater on pages 11–12.

MAKE THE BOOKMARK

2. Cut a 3½" x 6" (9cm x 15cm) rectangle from the sweater. Fold the felted apple-green sweater piece around the cardboard piece, covering the cardboard completely and pinning it in place.

3. Using aqua embroidery floss, blanket stitch around the two short ends and the long open side, taking the needle through both sweater layers and the cardboard.

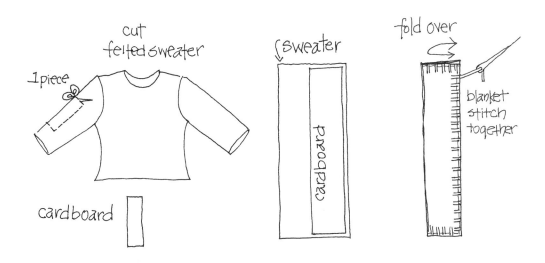

MAKE THE BEADED BEE

4. Thread one pink seed bead onto the center of a length of beading wire that is approximately 17" (43cm) long. Fold the beading wire in half with the pink bead at the center. You now have two wires to work with.

5. Bring the right wire to the left and thread it through two red seed beads. Bring the left wire to the right and thread it through the same two red seed beads. This will create a row of two red beads under the pink bead.

6. Bring the right wire to the left and thread it through three pink seed beads. Bring the left wire to the right and through the same three pink beads.

7. Bring the right wire to the left through two red seed beads and the left wire to the right through the same two red seed beads.

8. Bring the right wire to the left through three pink seed beads and the left wire to the right through the same three pink seed beads.

9. Bring the right wire to the left through four red seed beads and the left wire to the right through the same four red seed beads.

10. Bring the right wire to the left through five pink seed beads and the left wire to the right through the same five pink seed beads.

11. Bring the right wire to the left through three red seed beads and the left wire through the same three red seed beads.

12. Bring the right wire to the left through one pink seed bead and the left wire through the same seed bead. Twist the two wires together to secure the beading, bend wire ends to the back of the bee's body and snip off excess wire.

13. Take a wire length that is approximately 10" (25cm) long and secure it to the wire on the right side of the two-bead red row below the three-bead pink row. Twist the wire ends together to secure the tie. On the long wire end, thread thirteen red seed beads. Form the beaded area of wire into a loop for the right wing, and take the wire to the left through the two red seed beads of the body where you attached the wing wire. Thread on thirteen more red seed beads and form these in a loop for the left wing. Attach the wire end to the body wire on the left side of the two-bead red row, twisting the wire ends together to secure. Bend the twisted area to the back of the bee and snip off the excess wire.

ATTACH THE BEE TO THE BOOKMARK

add beaded bee

14. With a sewing needle and clear thread, sew the bee to the top of the bookmark, sewing through the wires on the ends of the bead rows.

FAIR ISLE CAMERA CASE

Keep your digital camera snug as a bug in its very own holder. Fair Isle, the knitting technique used to create the sweater from which you will felt, calls for the use of two or more colors to create intricate patterns. Typically, these patterns appear in the yoke of the sweater, with the remainder done in a solid color. This type of knitting originated in the northern islands of Britain.

Finished Measurements

3" (7.5cm) w x 4¾" (12cm) h

Materials

Fair Isle sweater made of mostly feltable fibers (see pages 10–11), at least 6¼" x 10" (16cm x 25.5cm)

Button Flower template (page 123) and tracing paper

Scrap of gold ready-made felt to fit template

1 skein size 25 purple embroidery floss

Beading thread

1 package of about 45 2mm seed beads in assorted colors

1 orange button, ⅕" (5mm) in diameter

1 green button, ⅗" (15mm) in diameter

 1 skein each Rowan Classic Cashsoft 4-ply yarn, 57% extra fine merino, 33% microfibre, 10% cashmere, 1.75 oz (50g), 197 yd (180m), in purple and royal blue

Small box of straight pins

DMC embroidery needle #5

Beadalon big eye beading needle 2¼" (5.7cm)

Tapestry needle

Size G-6 (4mm) crochet hook (optional)

Techniques

Washing and felting (pages 11–12)

Appliqué (page 116)

Embroidery: Backstitch (page 117), blanket stitch (page 116)

Crochet (optional): Slip stitch (page 118), chain stitch (page 118), double crochet (page 119)

cut
felted sweater

1 piece

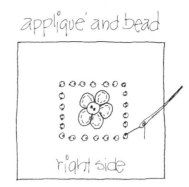

appliqué and bead

right side

FELT THE SWEATER

1. Follow the general instructions for washing and felting the sweater on pages 11–12.

APPLIQUÉ & EMBROIDER

2. Cut a 4¼" x 7" (11cm x 18cm) piece from the sweater. Lay the sweater piece flat with the 4¼" (11cm) ends at the sides and the 7" (18cm) sides at the top and the bottom.

3. Trace and cut out the template for the flower (page 123). Pin the flower template onto the gold felt, and cut it out. Place the felt flower in the center of the sweater piece.

4. Backstitch around each petal of the flower, using purple embroidery floss, to attach it to the sweater piece.

5. Using the beading needle and beading thread, sew the seed beads to the sweater piece in a 2½" (6.5cm) square around the flower, leaving a space about the width of a bead between each of the beads.

6. With purple embroidery floss, sew the orange button to the center of the flower. With purple yarn and the tapestry needle, sew the green button to the sweater piece directly above the bead square.

fold over

wrong side

sew

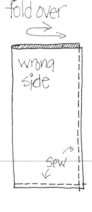

FINISH

7. Fold the sweater piece in half with right sides facing, bringing the 4¼" (11cm) ends together. The decoration will be on the inside. Machine-stitch or hand-sew the 4¼" (11cm) ends together, using a ¼" (6mm) seam allowance. Turn the piece right-side out.

8. Blanket stitch the front of the holder to the back across the bottom, using purple yarn and the tapestry needle.

9. Blanket stitch, using purple yarn and the tapestry needle, starting at the seam on the back and around the top edge of the camera holder. Unless you will be adding the optional crochet trim, tie off the yarn and trim off the excess.

embroider

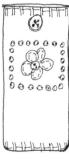

CROCHET TRIM (OPTIONAL)

10. Use purple yarn for the trim, either continuing with the yarn from the blanket stitches or attaching new yarn with a slip stitch. (Work 2 double crochet onto the nearest blanket stitch, chain 2, join the yarn to the next blanket stitch with a slip stitch); repeat the sequence in

parentheses all around the top of the holder. When you have reached the beginning, chain 32 to begin the loop, slip stitch into the 22nd chain to form the loop, work a single crochet in each chain from that point back to the edge of the holder. Join the yarn to the nearest blanket stitch, tie off, and weave in the end of the yarn.

CROCHET STRAP (OPTIONAL)

11. Twist purple and royal blue yarns together as one. Leave a 4" (10cm) tail and tie an overhand knot. Slip stitch the yarn to one upper corner of the camera holder, chain for 40" (101.5cm). Slip stitch to the other upper corner. Tie a knot with the yarn strands and cut, leaving 4" (10cm) tails. Tie an overhand knot with the chained strap (bringing the two sides of the strap together) 6" (15cm) from the top of the strap.

MINIATURE STOCKING ORNAMENT

It's never too soon to start thinking about the holidays. These tree ornaments are just waiting to be stuffed with tiny treasures and placed on your tree or above your fireplace. The stocking is made from a brightly colored mohair sweater.

Finished Measurements

3" (7.5cm) w x 5½" (14cm) h

Materials

Yellow-green sweater made of mostly feltable fibers (see pages 10–11), at least 8¾" x 16½" (22cm x 42cm)

Stocking template (page 122) and tracing paper

Sewing needle and yellow thread

1 SUPER FINE 1 skein each Rowan Classic Cashsoft 4-ply yarn, 57% extra fine merino, 33% microfibre, 10% cashmere, 1.75 oz (50g), 197 yd (180m), in light brown and dark green, plus fuchsia for crochet flower (optional)

Crocheted fuchsia five-petal flower (optional; see page 119)

Four 10mm nugget beads, 3 amber, and 1 translucent white (2 amber beads and the white one are optional)

Small box of straight pins

DMC embroidery needle #5

Beadalon big eye beading needle 2¼" (5.5cm)

Tapestry needle

Size G-6 (4mm) crochet hook (optional)

Techniques

Washing and felting (pages 11–12)

Embroidery: Blanket stitch, running stitch (page 116)

Crochet (optional): Slip stitch (page 118), chain stitch (page 118), single crochet (page 118), double crochet (page 119)

after cutting

(2 pieces)

sew

wrong side

FELT THE SWEATER

1. Follow the general instructions for washing and felting the sweater on pages 11–12.

MAKE THE STOCKING

2. Trace and cut out the Stocking template (page 122), enlarged at 200%. Pin the template onto the felted sweater and cut it out.

3. Pin right sides together. Machine-stitch around the sides of the stocking, using a ½" (13mm) seam allowance. Leave the top edge of the stocking open. Turn the stocking right-side out.

4. Turn under 1" (2.5cm) at the top of the stocking. Using light-brown yarn, the tapestry needle, and running stitch, stitch around the stocking to secure the top hem.

5. Blanket stitch around the machine-stitched edges of the stocking, using light-brown yarn and the tapestry needle.

APPLIQUÉ & EMBROIDER

6. If desired, you may crochet a five-petal fuchsia flower (page 119). Pin the crocheted flower in place on the front of the stocking. With the beading needle, sew an amber nugget bead in the center of the flower, simultaneously sewing the flower to the stocking front. Be careful not to sew the front of the stocking to the back while doing this. If you do not wish to use the crocheted flower, simply sew the amber bead to the front of the stocking at the same point where it would be if the flower were there.

CROCHET LOOP (OPTIONAL)

7. This loop will attach to the bead center of the flower, closing the stocking. Using dark-green yarn, join the yarn to the top center back of the stocking with a slip stitch. Chain 32, slip stitch into the 22nd chain to form the loop, work a single crochet in each chain from that point back to the edge of the stocking. Tie off the yarn and weave the end under the hem of the stocking.

CROCHET STRAP (OPTIONAL)

8. Using two strands of light-brown yarn held together, leave a 3½" to 4" (9–10cm) tail and tie an overhand knot with the two strands used as one. Attach yarn to the upper left corner of stocking (on the heel side). Crochet a 7" (18cm) chain. Chain 10 beyond the 7" (18cm) point. Form these 10 chains into a loop and slip stitch to the end of the 7" (18cm) chained strap. Sew an amber nugget bead onto the upper right corner of the stocking (on the toe side). The chained strap will come over the stocking and attach to this bead by the loop. At the end of the strand of yarn you left as a tail at the beginning of the strap, tie an amber bead. Tie the white translucent bead at the end of the other yarn tail.

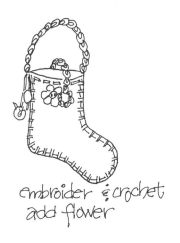

embroider & crochet
add flower

BOHEMIAN BOOK COVER

Protect your book or journal with this soft and colorful book cover. Design your cover to fit anything from the smallest book to a photo album or scrapbook.

Finished Measurements

To fit book you wish to cover

Size shown: 14" x 8¾"(35.5cm x 22cm)

Materials

Lime-green sweater made of mostly feltable fibers (see pages 10–11), at least 21" x 13.5" (53cm x 34cm)

Button Flower and Oversized Heart templates (page 123) and tracing paper

Scraps of ready-made felt in red, purple, and gold to fit templates

3 skeins size 25 embroidery floss to match red, purple, and gold felt

Sewing needle and red thread

2 green buttons, ⅕" (5mm) in diameter

1 yellow button, ⅗" (15mm) in diameter

Stiff woven fabric (such as linen), for lining, in turquoise, ½ yd

1 | SUPER FINE | 1 skein purple Rowan Classic Cashsoft 4-ply yarn, 57% extra fine merino, 33% microfibre, 10% cashmere, 1.75 oz (50g), 197 yd (180m)

Small box of straight pins

DMC embroidery needle #5

Tapestry needle

Size G-6 (4mm) crochet hook (optional)

Techniques

Washing and felting (pages 11–12)

Appliqué (page 116)

Embroidery: Blanket stitch (page 116), backstitch (page 117)

Crochet (optional): Slip stitch (page 118), chain stitch (page 118)

FELT THE SWEATER

1. Follow the general instructions for washing and felting the sweater on pages 11–12.

CUT OUT THE BOOK COVER

2. Lay your book open on the felted sweater and cut out the cover, allowing for an additional ½" (13mm) on all sides. (Your sweater piece will be 1" [2.5cm] longer and wider than your open book.)

3. Trace and cut out the templates for the Button Flower and the Oversized Heart, making two of the flower (page 123). Pin the heart template to the red felt, pin the first flower template to the gold felt, and pin the second flower template to the purple felt. Cut out the felt pieces.

APPLIQUÉ & EMBROIDER

4. With the sweater piece laying flat and the long sides at the top and bottom, the right-hand side will be the front of the book cover. Referring to the project photograph as a guide, position and pin the heart and the purple flower in place. Backstitch around each piece

cut felted sweater

open book

ribbed sweater

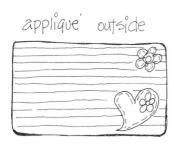

applique' outside

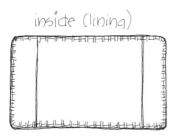

inside (lining)

⅛" (3mm) in from the edges, using matching embroidery floss, to attach the heart and flower to the sweater piece. Position and pin the gold flower on the heart. Backstitch around the flower to attach it to the heart, using matching embroidery floss.

5. Sew a green button to the center of each flower.

ASSEMBLE & FINISH

6. Lay the book cover on the woven turquoise fabric and cut out a lining the same size as your book. Also cut two pieces of woven turquoise fabric for flaps. They should be the same height as your book and 3¼" (8cm) wide.

7. Lay the sweater piece flat with the right side up. Then place the two flaps right side down on the ends of the sweater piece. Finally, add the larger lining fabric, matching the edges. Pin through all the layers to hold the cover and the lining in place. Machine-stitch or hand-sew around all edges, using a ⅕" (5mm) seam allowance; leave approximately 5" (12.5cm) unstitched in the center of one long edge for turning right side out. Turn right side out. Turn in the seam allowance in the unstitched area and whipstitch closed.

8. Blanket stitch around all edges, using purple yarn and the tapestry needle.

9. Sew the yellow button to the front of the book cover, approximately ¼" (6mm) in from the finished edge and in the center lengthwise, using purple yarn and the embroidery needle. As you attach the button, sew all the way through the lining but not through the flap.

10. Tie the yarn to the blanket stitch in the center of the back edge of the book cover. Make a 2" (5cm) loop and secure the yarn again to the blanket stitch on the center back edge. If desired, you can crochet the loop by slip stitching the yarn to the blanket stitch, chaining for approximately 4" (10cm), and joining the yarn again to the same blanket stitch. Tie off the yarn and weave in the end. The loop will slip over the yellow button on the front to keep the book closed.

11. To cover your book, insert the front and back covers of the book in the flaps of the lining.

HIP CELL PHONE HOLDER

Every cell phone should have one! Keep yours protected, cozy, and well-dressed with this simple-to-make, eye-catching cell phone holder. The one pictured is for a BlackBerry, but should fit most cell phones. To custom-fit your own, cut a piece of felted sweater the height of your phone plus ¾", and the width of your phone multiplied by 2 plus ¼".

Finished Measurements

2¾" (7cm) w x 5¼" (13cm) h

Materials

Cherry-red sweater made of mostly feltable fibers (see pages 10–11), at least 7½" x 8¾" (19cm x 22cm)

Scrap of blue denim fabric (try to find a scrap with a selvage)

Jeans template (page 122) and tracing paper

SUPER FINE 1 skein purple Rowan Classic Cashsoft 4-ply yarn, 57% extra fine merino, 33% microfibre, 10% cashmere, 1.75 oz (50g), 197 yd (180m)

1 skein size 25 denim blue embroidery thread

1 yellow button, ⅝" (16mm) in diameter

Approximately 30 2mm assorted seed beads, with 12 cobalt-blue and 7 yellow beads

Sewing needle and clear thread

Small box of straight pins

DMC embroidery needle #5

Beadalon big eye beading needle 2¼" (5.7 cm)

Tapestry needle

Size G-6 (4mm) crochet hook (optional)

Techniques

Washing and felting (pages 11–12)

Appliqué (page 116)

Embroidery: Blanket stitch (page 116)

Crochet (optional): Slip stitch (page 118), chain stitch (page 118), double crochet (page 119)

FELT THE SWEATER

1. Follow the general instructions for washing and felting the sweater on pages 11–12.

CUT OUT & EMBELLISH THE HOLDER

2. Cut a 6" x 5¼" (15cm x 13.5cm) piece from the felted sweater.

3. Place the sweater piece flat so that the 5¼" (13.5cm) edges are at the sides and the 6" (15cm) edges are at the top and bottom.

4. Trace and cut out the Jeans template (page 122). Pin the template onto the blue denim scrap. If you have a selvage on the scrap, place it at the bottom of the jeans. Cut out the jeans.

5. Place the jeans in the center of the sweater piece; pin it in place. Using blue embroidery floss, blanket stitch the jeans to the sweater piece around the inside of the legs, then up the outside of one leg, across the top, and down the outside of the other leg. Leave the bottom edges unattached. Using an embroidery needle, fray about ¹⁄₁₆" (2mm) across the bottom of each jeans leg.

6. Referring to the project photograph as a guide, sew a red-orange 2mm seed bead to the right of center of the jeans, approximately ³⁄₈" (10mm) down from the top edge. Sew seven yellow 2mm seed beads to the jeans, encircling the red-orange bead, to form the beaded flower.

7. Take a beading needle and thread up through the top left corner of the jeans from the back of the sweater piece. Thread on nine cobalt-blue 2mm seed beads to create the belt. Take the needle down through the jeans at the center left of the yellow bead flower and back up at the center right of the bead flower. Thread on three more cobalt-blue seed beads. Take the needle to the back of the sweater piece at the upper right corner of the jeans, knot and tie off the thread on the back of the sweater piece.

8. Randomly sew with beading needle nine or ten assorted colors of 2mm beads on the lower ¾" (2cm) of the left jeans leg.

9. Sew the yellow button just below the center top edge of the sweater piece.

ASSEMBLE & FINISH

10. Fold the sweater piece in half, bringing the 5¼" (13.5cm) edges together, with right sides facing (the decorations will be on the inside). Using a ¼" (6mm) seam allowance, machine-stitch across the 5¼" (13.5cm) edges. Turn right-side out.

11. Position the seam at the center back (the jeans will be centered on the front). Pin the front and back layers of the cell phone holder together near the bottom. Blanket stitch the bottom closed, using the purple yarn and the tapestry needle. Blanket stitch around the top edge.

CROCHET TRIM (OPTIONAL)

12. Start at the seam on the back and attach the purple yarn to the nearest blanket stitch with a slip stitch. (Work 2 double crochet onto the nearest blanket stitch, chain 2, join the yarn to the next blanket stitch with a slip stitch); repeat the sequence in parentheses all around the top of the holder. When you have reached the beginning, chain 32 to begin the loop, slip stitch into the 22nd chain to form the loop, work a single crochet in each chain from that point back to the edge of the holder. Join the yarn to the nearest blanket stitch, tie off, and weave in the end of the yarn.

appliqué

right side

fold over

wrong side

sew

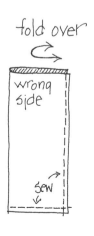

embroider

crochet

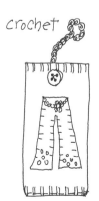

CHAPTER 2. FAST, FUN & FABULOUS:

INTERMEDIATE PROJECTS

The projects in this chapter are bigger in size and a bit more complex than those in the first chapter, but they're still very easy to make. You will be using larger pieces of felted sweater, but size and amount of shrinkage are not that important. Continue to experiment with shrinking your sweaters, and make sure to keep all the parts of the sweaters that you don't need for each project. Use the felted scraps for the appliqué parts on other projects in this book. Some basic sewing is required but can be done by hand or by machine.

FUNKY FELTED FLOWERED HAT

Funky meets function in this cute and stylish angora hat. No body heat can escape from this one. Its bright-orange color and fuzziness are sure to add a bit of fun to your wardrobe.

Finished Measurements

25¼ (64cm) circumference

Materials

Red-orange angora sweater made of mostly feltable fibers (see pages 10–11), at least 16" x 13" (40.5cm x 33cm)

Mini Heart and Leaf Pair templates (page 122) and tracing paper

Scraps of previously felted sweaters or ready-made felt in red, hot-pink, and avocado green (scraps work best), to fit the templates

 1 skein each Rowan Classic Cashsoft 4-ply yarn, 57% extra fine merino, 33% microfibre, 10% cashmere, 1.75 oz (50g), 197 yd (180m), in avocado green, light orange, beige, and white

Three 10mm amber beads

One 8mm black bead

Small box of straight pins

DMC embroidery needle #5

Tapestry needle

Beadalon big eye beading needle 2¼" (5.7cm)

Sewing needle and red sewing thread

Techniques

Washing and felting (pages 11–12)

Appliqué (page 116)

Embroidery: Blanket stitch (page 116), running stitch (page 117)

FELT THE SWEATER

1. Follow the general instructions for washing and felting the sweater on pages 11–12.

CUT OUT & EMBELLISH THE HAT

2. Referring to the illustration, cut two hat pieces from the felted sweater, using the bottom ribbed part of sweater for the hat bottom. The total height of each hat piece should be 11¼" (29cm): 6" (15cm) high for the cuff area, 2" (5cm) high for the area above the cuffs and before the slants, and 3¼" (8cm) high for the slanted area. The width of each piece should be 9" (23cm) up to the slants, then 4" (10cm) at the top.

3. Copy the Mini Heart (page 122) at 100% and again at 200%, to make two sizes of hearts. Trace and cut out the template for the Leaf Pair (page 122). Pin the larger heart template on the red felt and cut it out. Pin the smaller heart template on the hot-pink felt and cut it out. Pin the leaf pattern on the avocado-green felt and cut out five leaves.

4. Referring to the project photograph as a guide, pin the red heart and the leaves in position on the front piece of the hat. With avocado-green yarn, blanket stitch around each leaf to attach it to the front piece of the hat. With light-orange yarn, blanket stitch around the heart to attach it to the hat. Position the smaller heart on the larger heart. With beige yarn, blanket stitch around the smaller heart to attach it to the larger heart.

5. Cut a 3" (7.5cm) circle from the red felt. Using white yarn, the tapestry needle, and a running stitch, stitch around the edge of this circle approximately ¼" (6mm) from the edges. On the wrong side of the piece, in the center of the circle, stitch a ½" (13mm) circle with running stitches, using doubled red sewing thread and a sewing needle. Pull up these stitches tightly to gather up this area. Stitch through the gathers several times to secure. Knot and cut the thread. This gathered area on the back side of the red circle will make the circle look like a flower. Referring to the photograph as a guide, stitch the center of this flower to the front of the hat. Using the beading needle, sew the three amber beads and the one black bead in a cluster in the center of the flower.

MAKE THE HAT

6. Pin the two hat pieces together with right sides facing. Sew the pieces together around the edge. Turn the hat right side out and fold up the bottom approximately 2" (5cm).

7. Blanket stitch around the sides of the top of the hat, using two strands of beige yarn, held together, and the tapestry needle. Tie off the yarn and weave the ends in to the inside of the hat under a few blanket stitches.

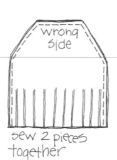

cut
felted angora sweater

2 pieces — ribbed bottom

sew 2 pieces together

fold bottom up

embroider blanket stitch & appliqué

2½"

FUNKY FELTED HEART PURSE

Felted sweaters make great fabric for purses. The sweater used in this project had some cables and patterns knitted in (all in the same color yarn), which made for a heavier and sturdier felted material. This purse is a great accessory for any outfit and it's sure to be a conversation starter. You may find that these purses are a lot like potato chips—bet you can't make just one!

Finished Measurements

13" (33cm) w x 10½" (26.6cm) h

Materials

Deep pink sweater made of mostly feltable fibers (see pages 10–11), at least 19½" x 20" (49.5cm x 51cm)

Wooden rectangular purse handles, 8½" x 3½" (21.5cm x 9cm) shown here

Mini Heart and Double Hearts templates (pages 122–123) and tracing paper

Ready-made felt or scraps from previously felted sweaters in deep pink and dark red, to fit templates

 1 skein each Rowan Classic Cashsoft 4-ply yarn, 57% extra fine merino, 33% microfibre, 10% cashmere, 1.75 oz (50g), 197 yd (180m), in deep pink and green

Approximately 40 iridescent white flower sequins

Approximately 40 size 10/0 seed beads in clear or light pink

Woven lining fabric, ½ yard

Beadalon big eye beading needle 2¼" (5.7cm)

Small box of straight pins

DMC embroidery needle #5 for appliqué work

DMC embroidery needle #18 to sew purse together

Tapestry needle

Size G-6 (4mm) crochet hook (optional)

Techniques

Washing and felting (pages 11–12)

Appliqué (page 116)

Embroidery: Blanket stitch (page 116), backstitch (page 117), lazy daisy stitch (page 117), backstitch (page 117)

Crochet (optional): Chain stitch (page 118)

FELT THE SWEATER

1. Follow the general instructions for washing and felting the sweater on pages 11–12.

CUT OUT THE PURSE

cut felted sweater

2 pieces

2. Per the illustration, draw a curved shape on the tracing paper that is 13½" wide (34.5cm) at the bottom, 7" wide (18cm) at the top, and 11" long (28cm), with an additional straight flap that is 7" wide (18cm) x 3" long (7.5cm). The total length should be 14". The flap will wrap around the handle and be sewn down to the inside of the purse, so the width of the flap should equal the inside width of the handles (here 7" [18cm]), and the length of it should be twice the thickness of the handles (here 3" long [7.5cm]); adjust the measurements of the flap to fit your handles. Cut out the paper pattern. Lay the pattern on the felted sweater and cut two pieces.

APPLIQUÉ & EMBROIDER

3. Trace and cut out the pattern for the Mini Heart (page 122) (enlarged at 400%) and trace and cut both of the Double Hearts (page 123), one using the larger outline as a template and the other using the smaller, interior outline as a template. Lay the template for the Mini Heart and the larger of the Double Hearts on the deep-pink felt and cut out one oversized heart and six of the double heart. Lay the smaller of the Double Hearts template on the dark-red felt and cut out six.

4. Referring to the project photograph as a guide, position the mini heart in the center of one side of the purse. Blanket stitch around the edge with matching-color yarn and the tapestry needle to attach the heart to the purse. Place the flower sequins over the entire heart area and hand-sew them to the heart, including a seed bead on top of each sequin, in the center.

5. Position the larger double hearts on the purse, as shown in the project photograph. Blanket stitch around each one to attach it to the purse, using the tapestry needle and matching-color yarn. Position the smaller contrasting double hearts on the center of each larger of the double hearts and blanket stitch each in place with matching-color yarn.

6. Embroider a stem to each double heart "flower," using a backstitch, the tapestry needle, and green yarn. Using a leaf-size lazy daisy stitch, embroider two or three leaves on each stem.

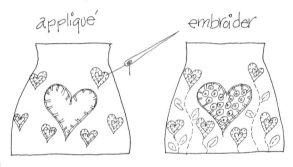

ASSEMBLE & FINISH

7. Turn the extension at each end of the purse through a purse handle, working from the outside to the inside of the purse. Hand-sew across the purse under each handle and through both layers, using a backstitch, the tapestry needle, and matching-color yarn.

8. Blanket stitch around the sides and the bottom of the purse, through both the front and back layers, using matching-color yarn and the tapestry needle.

9. Using a crochet hook, chain 6 (approximately) between each blanket stitch to make the corners fancier.

MAKE LINING

10. Lay the paper rectangle that you used to make the purse body on the lining fabric and cut it out, omitting the handle extensions. Fold the lining in half with right sides facing and stitch sides, using ¼" (6mm) seam allowance. Do *not* turn right-side out. Place the lining inside the purse. Turn under ¼" (6mm) across the top and whipstitch the lining to the top edge of the purse on the inside below the handles. Weave in any ends.

PATCHWORK SCARF

By stitching together two different-size rectangles from a felted sweater, you can make the scarf as long, or as short, as you like. Because the lamb's wool is extremely light, it makes sewing the rectangles together a breeze. This scarf is too beautiful to be worn only for functional purposes, and so soft you will never want to take it off! The scarf shown in the photograph was made from a floral-printed knitted sweater, but any plain or solid sweater will work just as well.

Finished Measurements

3¾" (9.5cm) w x 54½" (138.4 cm) l

Materials

Pale blue floral-print sweater or any lightweight lamb's wool sweater, plain or printed, size depending on the length of your scarf: a larger sweater will make a longer scarf, a smaller sweater will make a shorter scarf

Blanket Stitched Flower and Mini Heart templates (page 122) and tracing paper

Scraps of previously felted sweaters or ready-made felt in red-violet and purple, large enough to cover template for all flowers and hearts

1 skein each size 25 embroidery floss in deep pink and purple

 1 skein Rowan Classic Cashsoft 4-ply yarn, 57% extra fine merino, 33% microfibre, 10% cashmere, 1.75 oz (50g), 197 yd (180m), in olive green

1 orange button, ⅗" (15mm) in diameter

#10 DMC Cebelia Crochet Cotton in turquoise

Small box of straight pins

DMC embroidery needle #5

Tapestry needle

Size G-6 or H-8 (4mm or 5mm) steel crochet hook (optional)

108 aqua 2 mm seed beads (optional)

Techniques

Washing and felting (pages 11–12)

Appliqué (page 116)

Embroidery: Blanket stitch (page 116), running stitch (page 117)

Crochet (optional): Slip stitch (page 118), chain stitch (page 118)

FELT THE SWEATER

1. Follow the general instructions for washing and felting the sweater on pages 11–12.

MAKE THE PATCHWORK SCARF

2. Cut the large and small rectangular patches from the felted sweater. The large rectangles are 3¾" (9.5cm) x 4¼" (11cm); the small rectangles are 3¾" (9.5cm) x 2⅛" (5.4cm).

3. Position the patches as shown in the illustration, pin them, and hand-stitch them together using a running stitch and Cebelia yarn. Add one patch at a time, with right sides facing while stitching. For instance, sew the first two patches together with right sides facing. When you're finished, open out the new shape. Then add another patch, placing the right side of the new patch against the right side of the previously patched area. When finished, open out the new patched shape. Continue in this manner until the scarf is patched together.

APPLIQUÉ & EMBROIDER

4. Trace and cut out the templates for the flower (page 122) and the heart (page 122). Pin the flower on the red-violet felt and pin the heart on the purple felt. Cut out the felt pieces.

5. Referring to the photograph as a guide, pin the felt pieces in position on the scarf. Blanket stitch around the flower, using deep-pink embroidery floss, attaching the flower to the scarf. Repeat this process for the heart, using purple embroidery floss.

6. Using olive-green yarn, the tapestry needle, and running stitch, stitch a stem to the flower and to the heart.

7. Using the pink embroidery floss, sew the orange button to the center of the flower.

BLANKET STITCHED HEART AND FLOWER
APPLIQUES WITH RUNNING STITCHED STEMS

FINISH

8. Blanket stitch around the four sides of the scarf with the turquoise crochet cotton thread, starting on the left-hand corner of one short end. (If desired, you can use a crochet hook and chain 5 between each perpendicular part of the blanket stitch.) Tie off the thread unless you wish to add the optional crochet trim.

CROCHET TRIM (OPTIONAL)

9. Continue with the same thread used for the blanket stitch or join new thread (of the same type) to the blanket stitch with a slip stitch. (Chain 9, slip stitch to the next blanket stitch on the end of the scarf.) Repeat the sequence in parentheses across the scarf end. You will have made a row of chained "scallops" across the end. (Turn work. Chain 4, slip stitch into the center chain of the nearest the scallop on the previous row.) Repeat the sequence in parentheses for another row of scallops that is staggered with the previous row. Repeat this procedure for 19 more rows (each row is staggered with the row above it). Tie off thread.

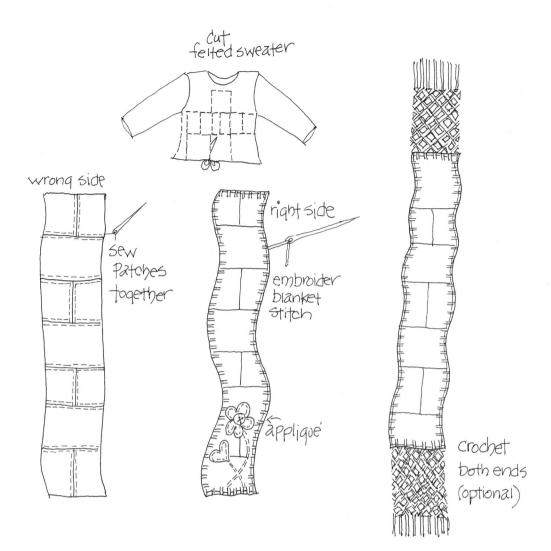

cut
felted sweater

wrong side

sew
Patches
together

right side

embroider
blanket
stitch

appliqué

crochet
both ends
(optional)

CHAINED AND BEADED FRINGE (OPTIONAL)

10. Thread 108 aqua seed beads onto the thread; you will bring them up to your work as you need them. Join thread to the outermost scallop on the left-hand side (the second to last row) with a slip stitch. (Make a chain that reaches to 1" [2.5cm] below the crocheted trim. Bring up 5 beads, then slip stitch to the chain above the first of these beads; this will draw the beads into a circle. Chain back up to the bottom row of trim. Slip stitch to the center chain of the nearest scallop, add a bead, and chain the same length as the chain from the beaded circle to the scallop.) Continue the sequence in parentheses across this end of the scarf. After the last circle of beads, chain up to the outermost right scallop on the second to last row of scallops, join with a slip stitch, and tie off thread.

11. Repeat on the other end of the scarf.

DOG-BONE DOG SWEATER

Dogs are man's best friends, so they have every right to wear one of man's best sweaters (an old one that's been felted, that is). And what dog (along with his owner) wouldn't want to prance around the neighborhood in a classy canine cardigan like this? The one shown here fits a fifty-pound Springer spaniel, but with a few quick measurements you can make one for any size pooch. A woman's sweater was used to create the felt for this project. For larger dogs, use men's sweaters. For smaller dogs, use children's sweaters. Also remember that this felted dog sweater is adjustable, depending on where you place the buttons. Make a scarf, on page 51, for your pup's best friend.

Finished Measurements

To fit measurements of your canine

Shown: Neck 7" (17.7cm)

Back width 12½" (31.7cm)

Chest width 7½" (19cm)

Overall length (back) 15" (38 cm)

Overall length (front) 13½" (34.3cm)

Materials

Woman's olive-green heather sweater made of mostly feltable fibers (see pages 10-11), at least 18¾" x 19½" (47.5cm x 49.5cm) (use a child's size for smaller dogs)

Blanket Stitched Flower, Vein Leaf, and Dog Bone templates (pages 122-123) and tracing paper

Scraps of ready-made felt in gold, lavender, cherry red, and kelly green, to fit templates

1 skein each size 25 embroidery floss in cherry red, lavender, gold, and yellow-green

1 orange and 1 yellow button, both ⅝" (16mm) in diameter

Four pink buttons, ⅝" (16mm) in diameter

Ten 2mm seed beads: 4 in green, 1 in red-orange, 4 in light green, and 1 in red

 1 skein each Rowan Classic Cashsoft 4-ply yarn, 57% extra fine merino, 33% microfibre, 10% cashmere, 1.75 oz (50g), 197 yd (180m), in olive green, pink, kelly green, and dark brown

5" (12.5cm) length of ribbon, ⅞" (22mm) wide, in a Byzantine or similar design

Small box of straight pins

DMC embroidery needle #5

Beadalon big eye beading needle 2¼" (5.7cm)

Tapestry needle

Size G-6 (4mm) crochet hook (optional)

Techniques

Washing and felting (pages 11-12)

Appliqué (page 116)

Embroidery: Blanket stitch (page 116), backstitch (page 117), straight stitch (page 117)

Crochet (optional): Slip stitch (page 118), chain stitch (page 118), single crochet (page 118)

FELT THE SWEATER

1. Follow the general instructions for washing and felting the sweater on pages 11–12.

CUT OUT & ASSEMBLE THE DOG SWEATER

2. Referring to the illustration as a guide, cut out two pieces from the felted sweater. The front is 12" (30.5cm) high, 13" (33cm) wide at bottom, and 4" (10cm) wide at top. Neckline is 8" (20.5cm) across. The back is 13½" (34.5cm) high, 13" (33cm) wide at bottom, and 10½" (26.5cm) wide at top. This will fit a forty-five– to sixty-pound (20–27kg) dog.

3. With right sides facing, match the shoulders of the two sweater pieces; pin them together. Machine-stitch or hand-sew the shoulder seams. Turn sweater back to the right side.

APPLIQUÉ & EMBROIDER THE DOG SWEATER

4. Trace and cut out the Blanket Stitched Button Flower, Vein Leaf, and Dog Bone templates. The Dog Bone template should be enlarged 200%. Place the bone pattern on gold felt and cut it out. Place the flower pattern on the lavender felt and cut it out. Then place the same flower pattern on the cherry-red felt and cut it out. Place the leaf pattern on the kelly-green felt and cut out two of them.

SEE HOW YOUR POOCH MEASURES UP!

To make one to fit your own dog, measure the width of your dog from shoulder to shoulder when he's sitting. This is the width you want the armholes to be in your felted sweater. This is the most important part of the fit. Generally, your shrinkage will be between 20 percent and 30 percent, so allow for that when you choose which sweater to felt. The placement of buttons will give you some flexibility in the fit, and the length can be adjusted and cut to fit as well. For very small dogs, use a baby or child's sweater.

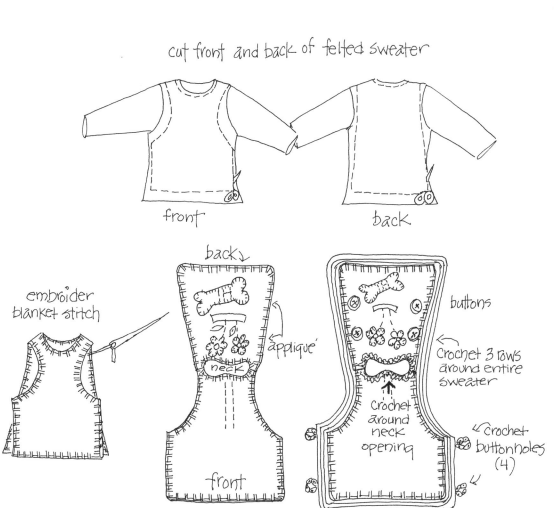

5. Referring to the project photograph as a guide, pin the felt appliqués in position on the sweater. Using matching-color embroidery floss, blanket stitch around the edges of the bone and the two flowers to attach them to the sweater piece. To attach the leaves, use yellow-green embroidery floss and backstitch up to the center of each leaf, attaching the center to the sweater piece. Embroider diagonal veins along the center veins, using straight stitch.

6. Using lavender embroidery floss, sew the orange button to the center of the lavender flower, adding four green seed beads in a circle on top of the button and one red-orange seed bead in the center of the green beads. Sew the yellow button to the center of the cherry-red flower, adding four light-green seed beads in a circle on top of the button and one red seed bead in the center of the green beads.

7. Using dark-brown yarn, the tapestry needle, and backstitch, embroider the word HI! on the bone.

8. Using kelly-green yarn, backstitch a 1¼" (3cm) stem on the sweater piece down from the lavender flower and a 2¾" (7cm) curved stem from the red flower.

9. Fold ¼" (6mm) under the two ends of the ribbon and pin the ribbon in place, centered on the sweater piece immediately under the bottoms of the embroidered flower stems. Topstitch the ribbon length to the sweater piece by hand or machine.

10. Using lavender embroidery floss, sew the four pink buttons where shown on the photo, to serve as closures.

FINISH

11. Fold under ¼" (6mm) around all edges of the dog sweater, including the neck opening; pin, if necessary.

12. Blanket stitch around the outer edges using the tapestry needle and olive-green and pink yarn held together. Using only olive-green yarn, blanket stitch around the neck opening. Tie off the ends and weave them under the hem, unless you plan to add the crochet trim.

13. On the bottom half of the dog sweater (the part that will be underneath the dog) sew yarn loops to the sides to match the pink button positions on the top part of the sweater. Using olive-green and pink yarns held together, size the loops to slip over the pink buttons. If desired, you can use a crochet hook and chain these loops as follows: Slip stitch yarn to the side of the sweater (either the blanket stitching or the optional crochet trim), chain approximately 10, form the chain into a loop and slip stitch to the side of the sweater again. Tie off yarn and weave in ends. Repeat at each loop position.

CROCHET TRIM (OPTIONAL)

14. Using olive-green and pink yarn held together, either continue with the yarn from the blanket stitching or attach new yarn to a blanket stitch with a slip stitch. Work single crochet onto the blanket stitch all around the outer edges of the dog sweater. When you reach the starting point, continue in a spiral manner for three more rows. Tie off yarn ends and weave them in. At the neckline, continue with the olive-green yarn from the blanket stitch or join new yarn with a slip stitch. Single crochet onto the blanket stitch, chain 6 all the way around the neckline, then work one final single crochet. Tie off the yarn and weave in the end.

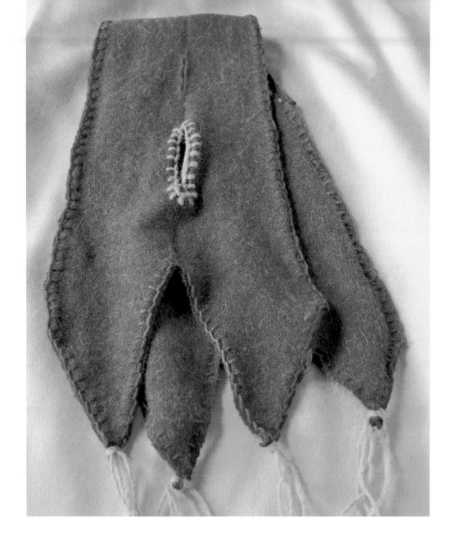

JESTER DOG SCARF

This cute Jester Scarf will make your dog feel warm and cozy—not to mention adorable—on those days when a sweater is just a little bit too much, but there is still a nip in the air. Make it from the sleeves of a sweater.

Finished Measurements

5¼" (13.3cm) w at center of scarf (width at ends of scarf 9" [22.8cm]) x 33" (83.8cm) l

Materials

Royal blue heather sweater made of mostly feltable fibers (see pages 10–11), with sleeves that measure about 23½" long x 6½" at the widest point (59.5cm x 16.5cm) (the sleeves should be sufficient)

 1 skein each Rowan Classic Cashsoft 4-ply yarn, 57% extra fine merino, 33% microfibre, 10% cashmere, 1.75 oz (50g), 197 yd (180m), in navy blue and yellow-green

Small box of straight pins

Tapestry needle

Techniques

Washing and felting (pages 11–12)

Embroidery: Running stitch (page 117), blanket stitch (page 116)

Lark's head knot for tassels (page 52)

FELT THE SWEATER

1. Follow the general instructions for washing and felting the sweater on pages 11–12.

MAKE THE SCARF

2. Cut out the two scarf pieces from the sleeves of the felted sweater, as shown in the illustration.

3. Overlap the two scarf pieces ½" (13mm), as shown, and stitch them together with yellow-green yarn, using a running stitch through both pieces.

4. Cut the slit for securing the scarf around the dog's neck.

FINISH

5. Using yellow-green yarn, blanket stitch around the slit.

6. Using navy-blue yarn, blanket stitch around the outside edges of the scarf.

TASSELS

7. Fold two strands of yarn in half and thread the *fold* through the tapestry needle. Take the yarn through the point on one end of the scarf. Holding the yarn in place, remove the needle. Bring the tails of the yarn through the loop made by the fold and pull tight. This is called a lark's head knot. Cut the tassel tails to approximately 3" (7.5cm) long. Make another lark's head knot right next to the first one at that same point of the scarf and in the same manner. Repeat on the other three points of the scarf.

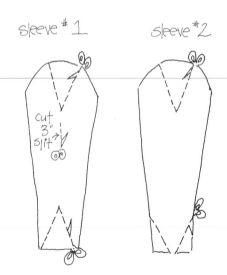

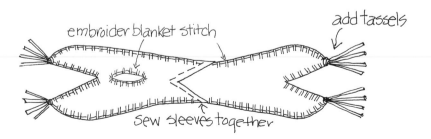

MESSENGER POUCH

When you don't need a regular purse, this pouch is perfect for carrying all your necessities. Made from a dark-violet sweater—the ideal backdrop for the potted flower appliqué—it features a bead closure and is fully lined. The bottom of the pouch is fringed in beads that have tiny bells dangling down.

Finished Measurements

5¼" (13.3cm) w x 7¼" (18.4cm) h

Materials

Dark-violet sweater made of mostly feltable fibers (see pages 10–11), at least 10" x 17½" (25.5cm x 44.5cm)

Double Flower, Vein Leaf, and Flowerpot templates (page 123) and tracing paper

Scraps made from previously felted sweater or ready-made felt in lavender, turquoise, green, and tan, to fit templates

1 skein each size 25 embroidery floss in aqua, lavender, yellow-green, and light brown

 1 skein each Rowan Classic Cashsoft 4-ply yarn, 57% extra fine merino, 33% microfibre, 10% cashmere, 1.75 oz (50g), 197 yd (180m), in red-violet, lavender, white, beige, turquoise, and yellow-green

1 orange button, ⅝" (16mm) in diameter

Approximately 100 2mm seed beads in assorted colors

One 18mm pink cylinder bead

12" x 7¼" (30.5cm x 18.5cm) piece of orange woven stiff fabric for lining

Beading thread

Nine 8mm jingle bells in assorted colors

Small box of straight pins

DMC embroidery needle #5

Beadalon big eye beading needle 2¼" (5.7cm)

Tapestry needle

Size G-6 (4mm) crochet hook (optional)

Techniques

Washing and felting (pages 11–12)

Appliqué (page 116)

Embroidery: Blanket stitch (page 116), backstitch (page 117), straight stitch (page 117), cross-stitch (page 117), backstitch (page 117)

Crochet (optional): Slip stitch (page 118), chain stitch (page 118), picot stitch (page 119), five-petal crocheted flower (page 119)

FELT THE SWEATER

1. Follow the general instructions for washing and felting the sweater on pages 11–12.

CUT OUT THE POUCH & EMBELLISHMENTS

2. Cut a 12" x 7" (30.5cm x 18cm) piece of felted sweater. Lay it flat with the 7" (18cm) edges at the sides and the 12" (30.5cm) edges at the top and bottom.

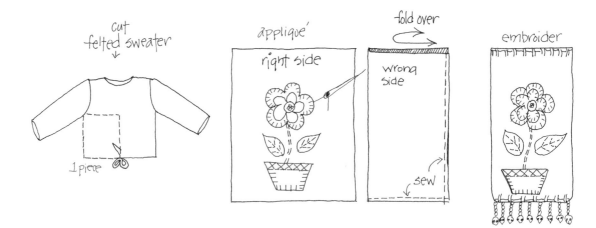

3. Trace and cut out the patterns for each of the Double Flowers, two Vein Leaves, and the Flowerpot. Pin the larger flower to the lavender felt, the smaller flower to the turquoise felt, and the flowerpot to the tan felt. Cut out one piece for each pattern. Pin the leaf to the yellow-green felt, and cut out two leaves.

APPLIQUÉ & EMBROIDER

4. Referring to the project photo as a guide, position the flowerpot and the lavender flower on the center of the felted sweater piece. Center the turquoise flower on the lavender flower. Using matching colors of embroidery floss and a blanket stitch, stitch around the flowerpot and the flower to attach them to the sweater piece. Across the top ⅜" (10mm) of the flowerpot, embroider a row of cross-stitches with the same color thread, then add a horizontal line of backstitches under the cross-stitches. Position the two leaves on the sweater piece, with the project photo as a guide, and, using yellow-green embroidery floss, embroider a line of backstitches up the center of each leaf to attach them to the sweater piece. Add diagonal veins on each side of the center veins with straight stitches.

5. Using yellow-green yarn and a running stitch, stitch a slightly curved stem from the flowerpot up to the flower.

6. Using embroidery floss, sew the orange button to the center of the flower. As you sew on the button, add four 2mm green seed beads on top of the button and one 2mm red seed bead in the center of the green beads.

MAKE THE POUCH

7. Fold the sweater piece in half with right sides facing, bringing the 7" (18cm) edges together; the decorations will be on the inside. Machine-stitch the 7" (18cm) edges together, using a ½" (13mm) seam allowance. Turn the pouch right-side out and position the seam at the center back.

8. Blanket stitch across the bottom of the pouch to close it, using red-violet yarn and the tapestry needle. Tie off the yarn and weave in the end. With the same color yarn, blanket stitch around the open top edge. Tie off the yarn and weave in the end.

CROCHET TRIM (OPTIONAL)

9. Continue with the same yarn from the blanket stitching in step 8, or tie on new yarn with a slip stitch. (Stitch 2 single crochet, then picot stitch.) Repeat the sequence in parentheses around the top of the pouch. Tie off the yarn and weave in the end.

FINISH

10. Sew the pink cylinder bead to the center front top of the pouch.

11. Sew a yarn loop onto the center front back of the pouch to fit over the bead on the front of the pouch. If desired, chain this loop.

MAKE THE LINING

12. Fold a 12" x 7¼" (30.5cm x 18.5cm) piece of orange woven fabric in half, with right sides facing, bringing the 7¼" (30.5cm) edges together. Machine-stitch or hand-sew the two layers of fabric together down the side. Position the seam at the center back, then stitch the two layers of fabric together across the bottom. Do *not* turn right side out. Place the lining inside the pouch, turn under ¼" (6mm), and whipstitch the lining to the inside top edge of the pouch.

MAKE THE BEADED DANGLES

13. Thread a beading needle with beading thread and knot the end of the thread. Take the thread from the inside of the pouch to the outside at the bottom edge. (Start at one bottom corner.) Thread six seed beads of assorted colors onto the thread, add a jingle bell, and take the needle back up through the beads and into the inside bottom of the pouch. On the inside, carry the thread over to the next point for a beaded dangle and repeat the process. Make nine beaded dangles, evenly spaced across the bottom of the pouch, ending at the opposite bottom corner.

STRAP

14. The strap is made with five strands of yarn—two strands of beige, one strand of lavender, one strand of turquoise, and one strand of red-violet. Allow for a 6" (15cm) tail, and tie an overhand knot with all these strands used together as one. Braid or (optional) chain the yarns for 42" (106.5cm). For a three-part braid, use two strands in two of the three groups and one strand in the third. For the optional chaining, use a crochet hook. Tie another overhand knot with all strands used as one, leaving a 6" (15cm) tail, and cut the yarns. Sew the overhand knots of the strap to the two upper corners of the pouch with a needle and thread. Tie a large overhand knot with the braided or chained strap at the very top of the strap, using both sides of the strap together as one.

CROCHET FLOWERS (OPTIONAL)

15. Crochet two beige five-petal flowers (page 119). Attach a flower to each upper corner on top of the overhand knots that begin and end the strap.

FAIR ISLE PURSE

After felting, a neutral-colored Fair Isle sweater makes a great everyday bag. The bright yarn embroidery provides a nice contrast and accentuates the intricate Fair Isle pattern. The bottom of the sweater (the ribbed part) becomes the top of the purse. Add a little beading, some wooden handles, and you're set.

Finished Measurements

16" x 11" (40.5cm x 28cm)

Materials

Sweater with a Fair Isle pattern made of mostly feltable fibers (see pages 10-11), at least 16" x 17.5" (40.5cm x 44.5cm)

 1 skein each Rowan Classic Cashsoft 4-ply yarn, 57% extra fine merino, 33% microfibre, 10% cashmere, 1.75 oz (50g), 197 yd (180m), in antique gold, red, green, fuchsia, and light gold

Eleven 14mm round amber beads

Approximately 140 4mm nugget beads in assorted colors

15½" x 23½" (39.5 x 59.5cm) piece of stiff woven lining fabric (such as linen)

Pair of wooden purse handles, 9" (23cm) wide, semicircles with holes for attachment

Small box of straight pins

DMC embroidery needle #5 for appliqué work

DMC embroidery needle #18 to stitch purse together

Beadalon big eye beading needle 2¼" (5.7cm)

Tapestry needle

Size G-6 (4mm) crochet hook (optional)

Techniques

Washing and felting (pages 11-12)

Embroidery: Blanket stitch (page 116), cross-stitch (page 117), backstitch (page 117), straight stitch (page 117)

Crochet (optional): Slip stitch (page 118), chain stitch (page 118)

FELT THE SWEATER

1. Follow the general instructions for washing and felting the sweater on pages 11-12.

CUT OUT THE PURSE

2. Cut two pieces of the felted sweater, as shown in the illustration. Each piece should be 11" (28cm) high and 15" (38cm) wide at the top, slanting to 12" (30.5cm) wide at the bottom.

APPLIQUÉ & EMBROIDER

3. Lay one piece flat with right side up and ribbing at the top, and work the following embroidery: Approximately 1" (2.5cm) below the ribbing, embroider a horizontal row of cross-stitches, using antique-gold yarn and the tapestry needle. Repeat 1½" (3.8cm) below the first row.

ABOVE, LEFT: THE PURSE IS EMBROIDERED WITH CROSS STITCHES AND ZIGZAGGING BACKSTITCHES, WITH STRAIGHT STITCHES FOR THE PETALS.

ABOVE, RIGHT: A ROW OF BLANKET STITCHES HOLDS THE TWO PIECES OF THE PURSE TOGETHER.

At approximately ½" (6mm) below the second row of cross stitches, embroider a zigzag row of backstitches with lavender yarn; make each backstitch ¾" (2cm) long and slant them in opposite diagonal directions. At 3¾" (9.5cm) below the zigzag row, repeat for another zigzag row. Between the antique-gold cross-stitch rows, embroider the flowers with four petals, using two strands of green yarn held as one and the tapestry needle, as follows: Use two straight stitches for each petal, one ⅝" (16mm) long and one ⅜" (10mm) long side by side, stitching these in each of the four diagonal directions. In the center of each, stitch a flower center with the green yarn using side-by-side straight stitches. Place the outside two flowers with the center about 2½" (6.5cm) from the edges and space the other two flowers evenly between them. Centered between the two red zigzag rows, embroider a row of five four-petal flowers with side-by-side straight stitches, as follows: Evenly space the five flowers across the width of the purse. Using fuchsia yarn and the tapestry needle, stitch a petal in each of the four directions (north, south, east, and west), using side-by-side straight stitches. Leave a space for the flower center. Using light-gold yarn and side-by-side straight stitches, stitch a circle for the flower center.

4. In the spaces between the green flowers (including outside the two outer flowers), sew a 14mm round amber bead. Sew a circle of assorted colors of nugget beads directly around each amber bead.

5. Repeat all embellishments on the other felted sweater piece.

ASSEMBLE & FINISH

6. Place the two decorated purse pieces together, wrong sides facing. Holding the fuchsia and light-gold yarns together, and using the tapestry needle, blanket stitch around the sides and the bottom to join the front and the back together.

7. Fold the lining fabric in half, right sides together, bringing the 15½" (39.5cm) sides together. These sides will be the top and bottom of the lining and will be left open at the top. Machine-stitch the two side seams, using a ¼" (6mm) seam allowance. Do *not* turn the lining right side out. Place the lining inside the purse, turn under ¼" (6mm) around the top edge, and whipstitch the lining to the inside top edge of the purse.

8. Sew the remaining 14mm amber beads at the center front of the purse, approximately ½" (13mm) down from the top edge. Make a loop with light-gold yarn and sew it to the top center back edge of the purse with the tapestry needle. If desired, you may crochet this loop as follows: Attach the light-gold yarn with a slip stitch and chain for the length of the loop; tie off the yarn and weave in the end. The loop will slip over the button at the top of the purse front for closure.

9. With the red yarn and the tapestry needle, sew the purse handles to the front and the back of the purse, through holes in the handles.

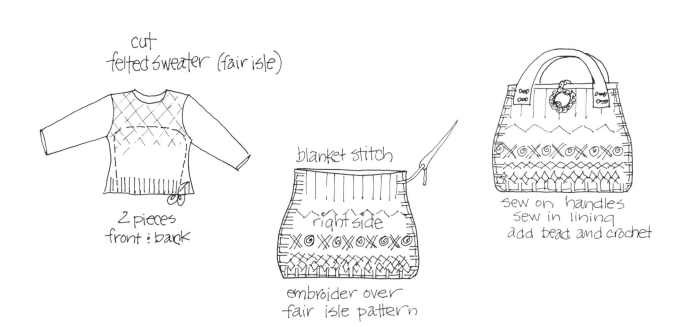

cut
felted sweater (fair isle)

2 pieces
front : back

blanket stitch

right side

embroider over
fair isle pattern

sew on handles
sew in lining
add bead and crochet

WINGED-HEART PILLOW

This beautiful pillow cover will be sure to add brightness, light, and color to any room in the house. Using pieces from three different sweaters, you can mix and match felt in an array of colors to go with just about anything and create nearly any size pillow. This is the perfect project if you have leftover scraps from other projects. The winged-heart appliqué adds a touch of whimsy.

~~~~~~~~~~~~~~~~~~~~~~~~~~~~~~~~~~

Finished Measurements

narrow pillows, at front:
17½" (44.5cm) w x 11" (28cm) h

Materials

Light-green sweater made of mostly feltable fibers (see pages 10–11), at least 15" x 16" (38cm x 40.5cm)

Button Flower and Winged Hearts templates (pages 123–124) and tracing paper

Scraps of previously felted sweaters in pink and light orange, for center pieces of pillow

20" x 11¼" (51cm x 29cm) piece of muslin

1 SUPER FINE 1 skein light-brown Rowan Classic Cashsoft 4 ply yarn, 57% extra fine merino, 33% microfibre, 10% cashmere, 1.75 oz (50g), 197 yd (180m)

Ready-made felt in purple, white, cherry red, and burgundy, to fit templates

1 skein each size 25 embroidery floss in pink, purple, cherry red, and burgundy

Two red-orange buttons, ½" (13mm) in diameter

Eight 2mm yellow seed beads

Two 2mm red-orange seed beads

22" x 11¼" (56cm x 29cm) piece of light-green woven fabric

Ready-made filler pillow, appropriate size for the cover, or fiberfill stuffing

Small box of straight pins

DMC embroidery needle #5

Tapestry needle

Techniques

Washing and felting (pages 11–12)

Appliqué (page 116)

Embroidery: Running stitch (page 117)

Basic sewing: Backstitch (page 117)

FELT THE SWEATER

1. Follow the general instructions for washing and felting the sweater on pages 11–12.

MAKE THE PILLOW FRONT

2. Following the illustration, draw a rectangle on the tracing paper that is 11" x 5½" (28cm x 14cm) to create the template for the side pieces of the narrow pillow. Lay this template on the light-green felted sweater and cut out two. Draw a rectangle that is 3½" x 6½" (9cm x 16.5cm) on the tracing paper to create the template for the top center and bottom center pieces. Lay the template on the pink felted sweater piece and cut two. Then draw a rectangle

that is 4" x 6½" (10cm x 16.5cm) on the tracing paper to create the template for the center piece. Lay the template on the light-orange felted sweater piece and cut out one.

3. Referring to the photograph, place the green sweater pieces on each end of the muslin backing. Between the green pieces, place the pink and orange pieces, with the orange piece in the middle. Pin the pieces in place. Turn under all the edges of the sweater pieces where they meet other sweater pieces so there are no raw edges.

4. Using light-brown yarn, the tapestry needle, and running stitch, sew around all sweater pieces approximately ¼" (6mm) in from the edges, sewing the sweater pieces to the muslin backing.

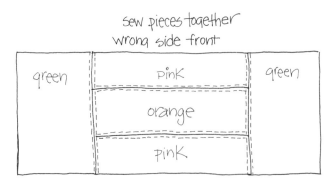

APPLIQUÉ & EMBROIDER

5. Trace and cut out the Button Flower template and each part of the Winged Hearts template (two hearts and two wings). Place the templates on the ready-made felt and cut out two purple flowers, one small cherry-red heart, one large burgundy heart, and two white wings.

6. Referring to the project photograph as a guide, position the felt flowers and the wings on the pillow front and pin them in place. Using pink embroidery floss for the wings and purple embroidery floss for the flowers, blanket stitch around each of the felt pieces to attach them to the pillow front. The large burgundy heart overlaps the inner side of each wing. Position the heart as shown in the project photograph and pin it in place. Blanket stitch around the heart with cherry-red embroidery floss to attach it to the front of the pillow. Center the cherry-red felt heart on the burgundy heart. Blanket stitch it in place with burgundy embroidery floss.

7. Using Cashsoft yarn, sew a red-orange button to the center of each flower. As you sew on the button, add four yellow seed beads on top of the button and one red-orange seed bead in the center of the yellow seed beads.

applique

THE FELTED SWEATER PIECES ARE SEWN TO THE MUSLIN WITH A RUNNING STITCH, AND THE WINGED HEARTS ARE BLANKET STITCHED TO THE PILLOW FRONT.

ASSEMBLE & FINISH

8. Cut a 7½" x 11" (19cm x 28cm) piece of the light-green woven fabric. Cut a 14½" x 11" (37cm x 28cm) piece of the light-green woven fabric. Turn ¼" (6mm) under one 11" (28cm) edge for each piece, then turn under ¼" (6mm) again, so you have turned under ½" (13mm) total on each piece. Machine-stitch or hand-sew each of these hems.

9. Lay the right side of each back piece on the right side of the pillow front with the hemmed edges of the pillow back toward each other. The back pieces will overlap each other approximately 1½" (3.8cm). Make sure the previously sewn hems are facing upward, not against the pillow front. Pin the pillow back and the pillow front together securely. Machine-stitch or hand-sew around all edges of the pillow, using a ½" (13mm) seam. Trim the seam allowance to ¼" (6mm). Cut closer diagonally across the corners, but not all the way to the seam. Turn the pillow right-side out through the opening where the hemmed edges overlap each other. Push out the corners well.

10. Insert the inner pillow or stuffing through the opening of the pillow back.

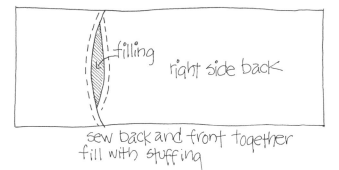

filling

right side back

sew back and front together
fill with stuffing

WOOLY BEAR

These cute stuffed animals are cut from felted sweaters, then sewn together and stuffed. You can add sweaters and scarves, or make your bear a whole wardrobe just by using different felted sweater scraps. This is also a soft, cuddly toy for babies and toddlers; just be sure to embroider the eyes instead of using beads if you're planning to give it to a young child.

Finished Measurements

9" (22.8cm) w x 12¼" (31.8cm) h

Materials

Heather gray sweater made of mostly feltable fibers (see pages 10–11), at least 13" x 18" (33cm x 46cm)

Turquoise sweater or already felted sweater scrap for bear's sweater

Wooly Bear, Wooly Bear Sweater, and Mini Heart templates (pages 122–124) and tracing paper

1 skein each size 25 embroidery floss in black, light brown, and lavender

Two 10mm round black beads for eyes

Polyester fiberfill to stuff bear

Scraps from previously made felted sweaters or ready-made scraps of lavender felt, for Mini Heart template

 1 skein Rowan Classic Cashsoft 4-ply yarn, 57% extra fine merino, 33% microfibre, 10% cashmere, 1.75 oz (50g), 197 yd (180m), in turquoise

3 turquoise buttons, ½" (13mm) in diameter, for sweater

A few yards of a multicolored variegated cotton yarn, for scarf

Small box of straight pins

DMC embroidery needle #5

Tapestry needle

Size G-6 crochet hook

Techniques

Washing and felting (pages 11–12)

Appliqué (page 116)

Embroidery: Blanket stitch (page 116), backstitch (page 117), satin stitch (page 117)

Crochet (optional): Slip stitch (page 118), single crochet (page 118)

FELT THE SWEATERS

1. Follow the general instructions for washing and felting the two sweaters on pages 11–12.

CUT OUT THE BEAR

2. Trace and cut out the Wooly Bear template, enlarged 200%. Cut the template into three separate parts—the ears, the head, and the body. Place the templates on the felted gray heather sweater and cut out two bodies, two heads, and four ears.

APPLIQUÉ & EMBROIDER

3. With black embroidery thread and referring to the project photograph as a guide, use back-stitches to embroider one of the head pieces with mouth lines. Embroider the nose with satin stitches. Sew the black beads in place for eyes.

ASSEMBLE & FINISH

4. Place the two body pieces together with right sides facing. Machine-stitch or hand-sew from one side of the neck around the arm, sides, and legs and up to the other side of the neck. Do not stitch across the neck. Turn the bear's body right side out and stuff with fiberfill.

5. Place two ear pieces together and machine-stitch or hand-sew around them, leaving the bottom open. Turn the ear right-side out. Stuff the ear with a small amount of fiberfill. Make the other ear in the same manner.

6. Place the two head pieces together, right sides together. You will create the face on the sides that are facing. Sandwich the ears upside down between the two pieces at the ear positions and pin in place; the tops of the ears will be facing downward and the edges of the head and the bottoms of the ears will be aligned. Starting on one side of the neck, stitch around the head to the other side of the neck, leaving the neck open. The ears will be attached in this process. Turn the head right-side out and stuff it with fiberfill.

7. Turn under the neck edges of the head and the body ¼" (6mm); pin this hem, if needed. With needle and gray thread, hand-stitch the head to the body around the neck.

MAKE THE SWEATER

8. Trace and cut out the Wooly Bear Sweater template twice, enlarged 200%. Pin the templates on the felted turquoise sweater and cut out two pieces for the front and the back.

9. Lay the piece that will be the back of the sweater right side up. Trace and cut out the Mini Heart template (page 122). Lay the heart on the lavender felt and cut it out. Position the felt heart on the lower right side of the sweater. Using lavender embroidery floss, blanket stitch around the heart to attach it to the sweater back.

10. Place the two pieces with right sides facing (the appliquéd heart will be on the inside) and stitch the shoulder seam, using a ¼" (6mm) seam allowance on all stitching for the sweater. On what will be the left shoulder seam (when turned right side out), stitch only the outer half of the seam to leave a placket so the sweater will fit over the bear's head. Stitch down each seam allowance in the placket area. Leave the armholes open. Starting at the bottom of each armhole, stitch each side seam. Turn the sweater right side out. Turn under ¼" (6mm) around the bottom, the neckline, and each armhole. Blanket stitch around all these areas, including the placket area of the neckline, using turquoise yarn and the tapestry needle. Tie off the yarn. Cut and weave in the end, unless you are going to insert the optional crochet edging around the neckline.

CROCHET EDGING (OPTIONAL)

11. Continue with the yarn from the blanket stitch or tie on new yarn with a slip stitch. Single crochet all around the neckline. Tie off the yarn; cut and weave in the end.

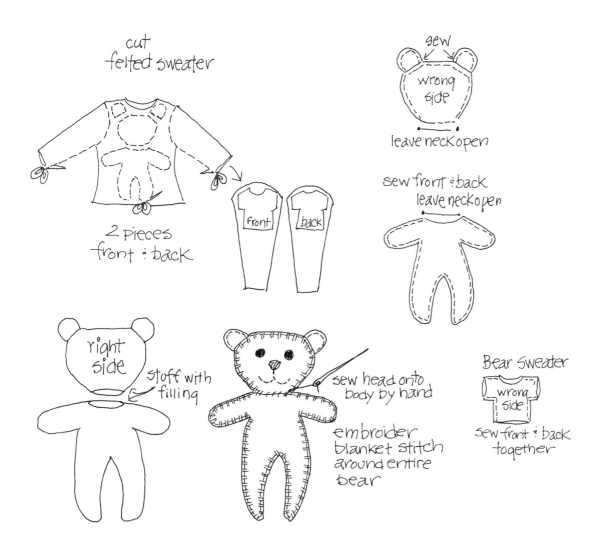

FINISH

12. Sew two turquoise buttons down the front of the sweater.

MAKE THE NECKLINE PLACKET CLOSURE

13. Using embroidery needle and Cashsoft yarn, sew the third turquoise button onto the front corner of the placket. Sew a yarn loop onto the back corner of the placket that will slip over the button. If desired, you can crochet this loop as follows: Join the yarn at the back corner of the placket with a slip stitch, chain enough for a loop, form the chain into a loop, and slip stitch again to the back corner of the placket. Tie off the yarn; clip and weave in the end. Place the sweater on the bear and button the neckline.

MAKE THE MULTICOLORED SCARF

14. Cut ten 21" (53.5cm) lengths of the multicolored variegated yarn. Place all the strands together, aligning the ends. Twist the whole bunch, and then fold it in half. Place the fold in front of the bear's neck and hold it in place. Take the ends around the bear's neck and then through the loop created by the fold. Let the ends hang down. For a solid wool scarf, wrap a piece of felted sweater around the bear's neck.

HELLO BABY HAT

This hat will keep your baby (or toddler) warm, cozy, and looking ever so cute. Custom-fit this piece to your little loved one's head. Just measure the circumference of his or her head—the width of each cut piece should be half the size.

Finished Measurements

19" (48cm) circumference

Materials

Purple sweater made of mostly feltable fibers (see pages 10–11), at least 9" x 11" (23cm x 28cm)

Straight Stitched Heart template (page 124) and tracing paper

Scrap of turquoise ready-made felt for template

1 skein size 25 embroidery floss each in turquoise and red

1 skein each Rowan Classic Cashsoft 4-ply yarn, 57% extra fine merino, 33% microfibre, 10% cashmere, 1.75 oz (50g), 197 yd (180m), in aqua, lavender, and beige

Beading thread

Approximately 30 2mm seed beads in assorted colors

Sewing needle and lavender thread

Small box of straight pins

DMC embroidery needle #5

Beadalon big eye beading needle 2¼" (5.7cm)

Tapestry needle

Size G-6 (4mm) crochet hook (optional)

Techniques

Washing and felting (pages 11–12)

Appliqué (page 116)

Embroidery: Blanket stitch (page 116), backstitch (page 117), running stitch (page 117)

Crochet (optional): Slip stitch (page 118), chain stitch (page 118), single crochet (page 118), double crochet (page 119)

FELT THE SWEATER

1. Follow the general instructions for washing and felting the sweater on pages 11–12.

APPLIQUÉ & EMBROIDER

2. Cut a 7½" x 11" (19cm x 28cm) piece from the felted sweater, as shown in the illustration. Lay the piece flat with the right side up and the 7½" (19cm) edges at the top and bottom. The bottom half of this piece will be the front of the hat.

cut felted sweater

1 piece

3. Trace and cut out the template for the heart. Lay the template on the turquoise felt and cut it out.

4. Referring to the photograph as a guide, position the heart on the sweater piece. Using turquoise embroidery floss and a running stitch, stitch the heart to the sweater piece.

5. Backstitch the word HELLO to the sweater piece in the lower right corner of the hat front, using red embroidery floss. Stitch an irregular rectangle around the word, using aqua yarn and a running stitch.

MAKE THE HAT

6. Fold the hat piece with right sides facing, bringing the 7½" (19cm) edges together. You will add the decorations on the inside. Using a ¼" (6mm) seam allowance, machine-stitch or hand-sew the two layers together on the sides. The fold will be at the top of the hat. Turn the hat right-side out.

7. Using lavender yarn and a running stitch, stitch down the seam allowances of the side seams approximately ⅛" (3mm) on each side of the seams.

8. Turn up the bottom edge of the hat ¼" (6mm). Blanket stitch around the bottom edge of the hat, using lavender and beige yarn, held together, and the tapestry needle. Tie off the yarn and weave the ends under the hem, unless you plan to add the optional crochet trim.

CROCHET TRIM (OPTIONAL)

9. Continue with the yarns from the blanket stitching or attach new yarns with a slip stitch. (Single crochet onto blanket stitch, work two double crochet onto the blanket stitch, work one single crochet onto the blanket stitch, slip stitch onto the blanket stitch.) Continue the sequence in parentheses all around the edge of the hat. Tie off the yarn; clip and weave in the ends.

MAKE THE PINCHED CORNERS

10. Thread 15 assorted colors of 2mm seed beads onto the beading thread. Tie the ends of the thread together tightly so that the beads form a circle. Take the thread ends back through a few beads to hide them and clip off the thread. Pull one upper corner of the hat through the bead circle for approximately 1" (2.5cm). With a sewing needle and lavender thread, tack the bead ring to the hat in a few places to secure it. Repeat with the other top corner of the hat.

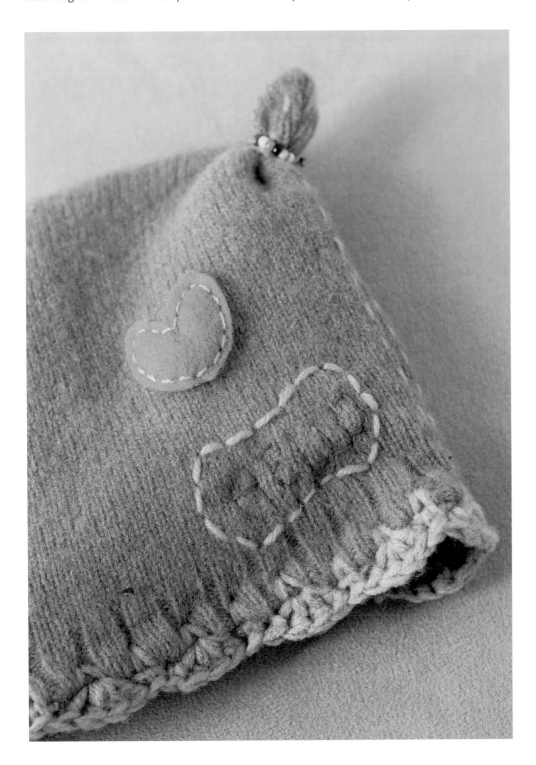

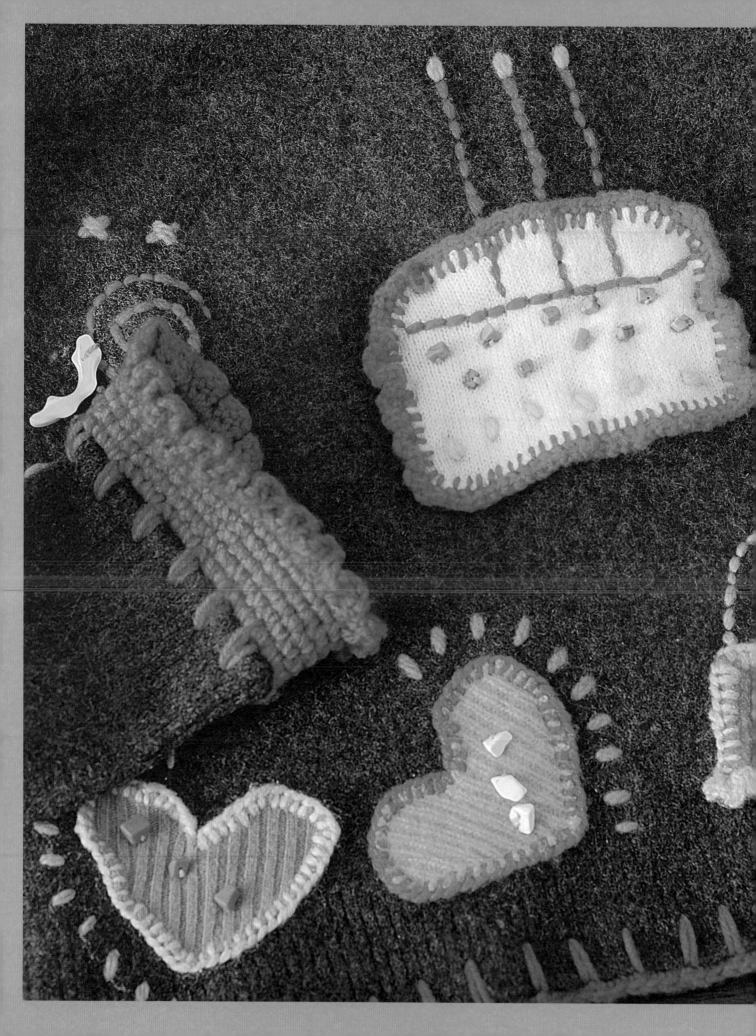

ADVANCED PROJECTS

The projects in this chapter are actual sweaters (and a skirt) made from your felted sweaters. Sizing is very important here. You should try a few projects from the first or second chapter before you begin one of these. The overall size of the sweater—before felting and afterward—is crucial. Start with a sweater that is one to three sizes too big, and be sure to felt it using short wash cycles. Keep washing it until you achieve the desired size. Since you don't want it to shrink any more, dry it on a no-heat setting.

SUGAR & SPICE SWEATER

Everyone loves cozy, comfortable sweaters, especially little girls. This short-sleeve mock turtleneck is made from a sweater that combines a mix of mohair, angora, and lamb's wool. The felting process leaves the fiber soft, with no itchiness. The front and back of the sweater are appliquéd with apparel motifs, which are embellished with beads.

If you are not experienced with the felting process, I recommend making a couple of accessory projects before trying a sweater project like this, as you will need some practice in washing and felting before making a project where size is crucial.

Finished Measurements

Neck width 6" (15.2cm) x 2" (5cm) h

Shoulder width 11½" (29.2cm)

Sleeve length 4¾" (12cm)

Overall length 18" (45.7cm)

Overall width 13" (33cm)

Materials

Pink sweater—made from mohair, angora, or lamb's wool—at least 25% larger than finished size

Pants, Heart Sweater, Mini Sweater, and Jean Skirt templates (pages 122–125) and tracing paper

Ready-made felt or previously felted sweater scraps in denim blue, deep pink, turquoise, hot pink, olive green, and black to fit templates

8½" x 11" (21.5cm x 28cm) cardboard rectangle to put inside sweater while working

1 skein size 25 embroidery floss each in blue, deep pink, aqua, yellow-green, and yellow

Tiniest size seed beads (smaller than 10/0), approximately 30 of one color and 20 of second color

Ten 4mm plastic faceted beads

Four 2-hole flat buttons, ⅜" to ½" (10–13mm) in diameter

 1 skein each Rowan Classic Cashsoft 4-ply yarn, 57% extra fine merino, 33% microfibre, 10% cashmere, 1.75 oz (50g), 197 yd (180m), in deep pink and light brown

Beadalon big eye beading needle 2¼" (5.7cm)

Small box of straight pins

DMC embroidery needle #5

Tapestry needle

Size G-6 (4mm) crochet hook (optional)

Techniques

Washing and felting (pages 11–12)

Appliqué (page 116)

Embroidery: Blanket stitch (page 116), straight stitch (page 117), baskstitch (page 117)

Crochet (optional): Chain stitch (page 118), single crochet (page 118)

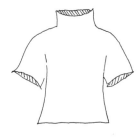

felted
sweater

FELT THE SWEATER

1. Follow the general instructions for washing and felting the sweater on pages 11–12.

APPLIQUÉ & EMBROIDER

2. Trace and cut out the templates for the motifs (pages 122–125), cutting out the heart separate from the Heart Sweater and making two templates of the Mini Sweater. Lay the Pants template on the denim-blue felt, the Heart Sweater on the deep-pink felt, the Heart on the turquoise felt, one Mini Sweater on the hot-pink felt, the other Mini Sweater on the olive-green felt, and the Jean Skirt on the black felt. Cut them all out.

3. Place the cardboard inside the sweater to avoid sewing the front to the back.

4. Position the pants on the front of sweater, placing the heart sweater slightly above it. Position the heart in the center of the heart sweater. Pin all motifs in place.

front
appliqué

5. Blanket stitch around each piece to attach it to the sweater, using blue embroidery floss for the jeans, deep-pink floss for the shirt, and aqua for the heart.

6. Outline the beaded zipper and beaded pocket edges of the pants with strands of tiny seed beads of one color, using the photo as a guide (opposite page, bottom left). Outline this first row of beads with the second color of seed beads. If larger seed beads are used, only one line is needed for each area.

7. Make the belt for the pants with two strands of blue embroidery floss held together as one. Bring the floss up on each side of the slacks at belt level from the inside of the sweater. Take the floss across the pants to the right side. Tie the floss ends together with an overhand knot. Thread a plastic faceted bead on each floss end and tie an overhand knot under each bead to hold it in place.

8. On the back of the sweater, pin the felt jean skirt and the mini sweaters in place side by side, with the skirt in the middle. Blanket stitch around the deep-pink mini sweater, using matching-color embroidery floss to attach it to the sweater. Repeat for the skirt, using blue embroidery floss, and for the olive-green shirt, using yellow-green embroidery floss.

back
appliqué

9. Using yellow embroidery floss, embellish one mini sweater with a row of embroidered crosses at the underarm level, each made with a straight stitch in each of four directions from a single point. Embellish the skirt with a row of three yellow embroidered crosses. On the mini sweater, make a small stitch through the shirt at the center neckline. Thread a plastic faceted bead on each thread end and secure each bead with an overhand knot underneath.

10. Using a chain stitch, embroider a 6" x 2¾" (15cm x 7cm) rectangle around the two mini sweaters and the skirt on the back of the sweater using light-brown yarn. Using the embroidery needle, sew a button onto each corner of the rectangle, threading a plastic faceted bead onto the thread before taking it down through the second hole. Knot the thread on the inside of the sweater.

FINISH

11. This pattern calls for a short-sleeve sweater, but a long-sleeve sweater can be cut to the desired sleeve length after felting. Cut sleeve to correct length, roll in the edge, and whipstitch.

blanket stitch
or
crochet edges

12. Blanket stitch around the sweater's edges with deep-pink embroidery floss. You can also crochet around the edges with a single crochet stitch, or chain a few stitches between each blanket stitch.

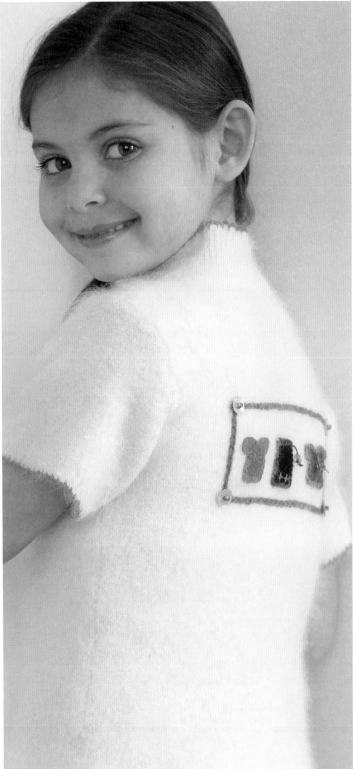

ABOVE, LEFT: ON THE BACK OF THE SWEATER, TWO CROSSES ARE STRAIGHT STITCHED TO THE SWEATER AND SKIRT APPLIQUÉS. A RECTANGULAR BORDER IS CHAIN STITCHED AROUND ALL THREE APPLIQUÉD PIECES, AND A BUTTON IS SEWN TO EACH CORNER.

BELOW, LEFT: THE SWEATER AND PANTS APPLIQUÉS ARE BLANKET STITCHED TO THE FRONT OF THE SWEATER.

FLOWER POWER KID'S CARDIGAN

Adorable with a dress or skirt, this is the perfect little cardigan to match just about any outfit. You can even pair it with jeans and a T-shirt. And the bright felted and beaded flowers are sure to make any little girl smile.

Finished Measurements

Neck width 7½" (19cm)

Shoulder width 14" (35.5cm)

Sleeve length 16½" (40.6cm)

Overall length 16" (40.6cm)

Overall width 15" (38cm)

Materials

Turquoise sweater made of mostly feltable fibers (see pages 10-11), at least 25% larger than finished size

Button Flower, Double Flower, and Half Flower templates (pages 123, 125) and tracing paper

Scraps of ready-made felt or previously felted sweaters in lavender, red-violet, light orange, light green, and purple, to fit templates

1 skein size 25 embroidery floss each in lavender, light green, and deep pink

1 package 2mm seed beads in assorted colors

4 buttons, ⅜" (10mm) in diameter in assorted colors

1 green button, ⅝" (16mm) in diameter

Four 3mm cream-colored seed beads

 1 skein Rowan Classic Cashsoft 4-ply yarn, 57% extra fine merino, 33% microfibre, 10% cashmere, 1.75 oz (50g), 197 yd (180m), in turquoise, dark green, and light green

2 brown buttons for sweater closure, ¾" (2cm) in diameter

Small box of straight pins

DMC embroidery needle #5

Beadalon big eye beading needle 2¼" (5.7cm)

Tapestry needle

Size G-6 (4mm) crochet hook (optional)

Techniques

Washing and Felting (pages 11-12)

Appliqué (page 116)

Embroidery: Blanket stitch (page 116), running stitch (page 117), straight stitch (page 117)

Crochet (optional): Chain stitch (page 118), single crochet (page 118)

FELT THE SWEATER

1. Follow the general instructions for washing and felting the sweater on pages 11-12.

MAKE THE CARDIGAN

2. To turn the felted sweater into a cardigan, cut up through the front of the sweater as shown in the illustration. Then cut out the neck, ends of sleeves, and bottom of sweater. Turn all edges under ½" (13mm) and sew with a running stitch.

cut
felted sweater

applique'

back

turn edges under
and sew

blanket stitch

applique'
and embroider

crochet
add button

3. Using turquoise and light-green yarn held together, blanket stitch around the entire edge of the sweater.

APPLIQUÉ & EMBROIDER

4. Trace and cut out the templates for the Button Flower five times (page 123). Pin the flowers to the different colors of felt and cut them out. Also cut out one Half Flower in lavender and one half-center in orange for the Half Flower. Trace and cut out the templates for the Double Flower. Pin the larger flower to the red-violet felt and the smaller flower to the orange felt. Position the felt flowers on the sweater, as shown in the illustration, and pin in place. Blanket stitch around the felt flowers to attach them to the sweater, using matching-color embroidery floss. Place the orange felt half-center on the half-flower. Using a running stitch and orange embroidery floss, stitch around the center to attach it to the half-flower. Place the small orange flower on the large red-violet flower on the back of the sweater. Using a running stitch and light-green embroidery floss, stitch around each petal to attach it to the larger flower.

5. Sew assorted colors of 2mm seed beads over the entire flower center of the half-flower.

6. Sew a ⅜" (10mm) button to the center of each remaining flower on the front and the sleeve. Sew the ⅝" (16mm) button to the center of the double flower on the back of the sweater; thread the four 3mm cream-colored beads onto the lavender yarn as you sew on the button.

7. Using a running stitch, sew assorted colors of 2mm seed beads in an outline of a heart around the double flower on the back of the sweater. Thread on one bead at a time in order to leave a little extra space between beads.

8. On the sleeve, following the diagram, stitch a running stitch with dark-green yarn and the tapestry needle for a stem that connects the flowers.

9. Sew the ¾" (2cm) button onto one upper corner of front with turquoise yarn. On the other upper corner, attach a loop with turquoise yarn that will fit over the button as a closure. If you wish, you may chain stitch this loop.

CROCHET EDGING (OPTIONAL)

10. Attach the turquoise and light-green yarns, held together, onto the blanket stitch with a slip stitch. Single crochet onto the blanket stitches all around the sweater. Single crochet in each single crochet for five more rows. Tie off the yarn and weave in the yarn ends.

THE RED-VIOLET FLOWER IS BLANKET STITCHED TO THE BACK OF THE SWEATER, AND THE SMALL ORANGE FLOWER IS SEWN ON TOP WITH A RUNNING STITCH.

BIRTHDAY SWEATER

Every day will feel like your birthday when you're wearing this festive sweater. Colorful and fun, it will bring a smile to you and everyone you meet while you're wearing it. Hearts, flowers, and a big birthday cake, complete with candles, make a great contrast to the gray background. The bright red crochet trim adds the finishing touch.

Finished Measurements

Neck 10" (25.9cm)

Shoulder width 16" (40.6cm)

Sleeve length 18" (45.7cm)

Overall length 17½" (44.4cm)

Overall width 17½" (44.4cm)

Materials

Charcoal sweater made of mostly feltable fibers (see pages 10-11), at least 25% larger than finished size

Birthday Cake, Birthday Heart (copied at 200%), **Birthday Teacup, Birthday Purse,** and **Mini Heart templates** (pages 122, 125) and tracing paper

Scraps of previously felted sweaters or ready-made felt in white, light green, light orange, orange, dusty rose, cherry red to fit templates

Rectangle of cardboard the size of the felted sweater body

1 skein each Rowan Classic Cashsoft 4-ply yarn, 57% extra fine merino, 33% microfibre, 10% cashmere, 1.75 oz (50g), 197 yd (180m), in cherry

red, light orange, white, aqua, pink, fuchsia, red-violet, gold, yellow, green; light green for optional crocheted flower

Nugget beads, approximately 5mm to 6mm, in white (7 beads), orange (3 beads), turquoise (14 beads)

Plastic "mother of pearl" sliver beads: white (1 bead), pink (3 beads)

DMC embroidery needle #5

Beadalon big eye beading needle 2¼" (5.7cm)

Tapestry needle

Size G-6 (4mm) crochet hook (optional)

Techniques

Washing and felting (pages 11-12)

Appliqué (page 116)

Embroidery: Blanket stitch (page 116), **straight stitch** (page 117), **backstitch** (page 117), **cross-stitch** (page 117), **satin stitch** (page 117)

Crochet (optional): Slip stitch (page 118), **chain stitch** (page 118), **single crochet** (page 118), **double crochet** (page 119)

FELT THE SWEATER

1. Follow the general instructions for washing and felting the sweater on pages 11-12.

BLANKET STITCH THE EDGES

2. Cut out the neck, hem, and cuffs of the sweater as shown in the illustration. Turn all edges under ½" (13mm) and sew with a running stitch. Blanket-stitch the bottom edge with cherry-red yarn and the tapestry needle; blanket stitch around the neck and the cuffs using cherry-red and light-orange yarns held together.

APPLIQUÉ

3. Trace and cut out the templates for the decorations, making two Birthday Heart templates. Lay the templates on the felted sweater scraps and cut out as follows: Birthday Cake, white; Birthday Heart, light green; Birthday Heart, light orange; Birthday Purse, orange; Birthday Teacup, dusty rose.

4. Insert the cardboard into the sweater to avoid sewing the front to the back.

5. On the sweater front, position the birthday cake, the two smaller hearts, and the purse and teacup as shown in the photograph. Blanket stitch each one to the sweater around each appliqué, using the tapestry needle. Use the following colors of yarn: cherry red around the white birthday cake, white around the smaller green heart, fuchsia around the smaller light-orange heart, pink around the orange purse, and cherry red around the dusty-rose purse.

CROCHET EDGING (OPTIONAL)

6. If desired, edge the birthday cake with single crochets stitched onto the blanket stitches. If desired, add a row of single crochets across the bottom of the orange purse, stitching as many as you can onto the blanket stitches across the bottom so this edging will ruffle. You may also crochet a flower with light-green yarn (page 119) and tie it to the orange purse.

EMBROIDER

7. Refer to the project photo and embroider as follows:

- Backstitch a curved line to suggest the front edge of the birthday cake with the same color yarn as the edging of the appliqué.
- Backstitch three candles with fuchsia yarn from the front edge of the cake upward to approximately 2" (5cm) above the cake. On each candle, satin stitch a flame with gold yarn.
- Backstitch a handle onto the top of the orange purse with aqua yarn. At the top of the handle, satin stitch two bow loops.
- Backstitch a handle onto the right side of the dusty-rose purse with blue yarn.
- Backstitch a spiral onto the sweater with cherry-red yarn and another spiral with aqua yarn.

8. Refer to the project photo and embroider the following straight stitches:

- Using aqua yarn and the tapestry needle, embroider eleven "radiating" straight stitches around the left side of the green heart.
- Using orange yarn, embroider ten "radiating" straight stitches around the right side of the orange heart.
- Using yellow yarn, embroider three random straight stitches between the two purses.
- Using yellow yarn, embroider six vertical straight stitches across the bottom of the birthday cake.

9. Refer to the project photo and embroider cross-stitches in the following areas:

- With gold yarn and the tapestry needle, embroider a diagonal row of four cross-stitches below the red spiral.
- With green yarn, embroider a diagonal row of two cross-stitches above the red spiral.

- With gold yarn, embroider a vertical row of four cross-stitches below and to the right of the aqua spiral.
- With green yarn, embroider a horizontal row of two cross-stitches above the aqua spiral.

10. Referring to project photo, sew two horizontal rows of five turquoise nugget beads each across the top of the birthday cake below the front edge of the cake. Stagger the beads on the lower row with those on the row above.

11. Sew a diagonal row of three orange nugget beads across the green heart.

12. Sew a diagonal row of three white nugget beads across the orange heart.

13. Sew a horizontal row of four turquoise nugget beads across the top of the dusty rose purse.

14. Refer to project photo and sew the sliver beads to the following areas: a white sliver on the red spiral, a pink sliver on the aqua spiral, and a pink sliver to top of the handle of each purse.

15. Copy the template for the Birthday Heart at 200%. Lay the template on the cherry-red felted sweater piece and cut out the heart.

16. Position the heart on the center back of the sweater. Blanket stitch around the heart, with yellow yarn and the tapestry needle, to attach the heart to the sweater

17. Using cherry-red yarn and the tapestry needle, embroider thirteen "radiating" straight stitches around the right side of the heart.

18. Using fuchsia yarn and the tapestry needle, embroider a vertical row of four cross-stitches below the heart.

19. Sew a diagonal row of four white nugget beads across the heart.

CROCHET NECKLINE & CUFFS (OPTIONAL)

20. If desired, add crochet trim around the neck and the cuffs. Attach cherry-red and light-orange yarns, held together, to blanket stitch (or continue with the same yarn from the blanket stitching) and work single crochets onto the blanket stitches all the way around the neckline and the cuffs. Single crochet four more rounds around the neckline and five more rounds around each cuff. Continue around the cuffs with only the cherry-red yarn as follows: (Single crochet in one stitch; chain 4, skip a stitch, double crochet in the next stitch 3 times; chain 3, skip one stitch) all the way around the cuff. Tie off the yarn and weave the tails to the inside. Repeat on the other cuff.

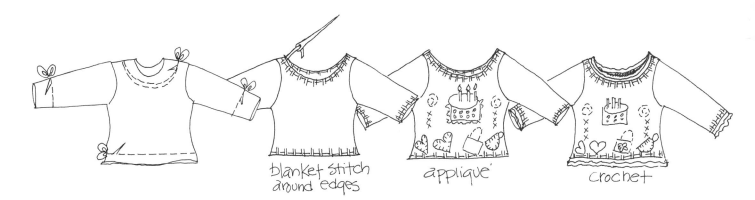

blanket stitch around edges

applique

crochet

FLOWERED CARDIGAN

This cardigan is classic—with a twist. When the leaves start to change, this casual but fun-looking, jewel-toned piece will fit right in.

Finished Measurements

Neck width 8" (20.3cm)

Shoulder width 16" (40.6cm)

Sleeve length 23½" (59.7cm)

Overall length 19" (48.3cm)

Overall width 19" (48.3cm)

Materials

Burgundy sweater made of mostly feltable fibers (see pages 10–11), at least 25% larger than finished size

Pants, Button Flower, Mini Sweater, Double Circles templates (pages 123–125) and tracing paper

Scraps of previously felted sweaters or ready-made felt in lavender, gold, peach, cherry red, red-orange, magenta, beige, and aqua, to fit templates

1
SUPER FINE 1 skein each Rowan Classic Cashsoft 4-ply yarn, 57% extra fine merino, 33% microfibre, 10% cashmere, 1.75 oz (50g), 197 yd (180m), in fuchsia, beige, light brown, and avocado green

1 skein size 25 embroidery floss each in gold, aqua, beige purple, fuchsia, cherry red, red-orange, peach, lime green, light brown, and brown

1 red, 1 white, and 1 orange button, all ½" (13mm) in diameter

Approximately 125 2mm seed beads in assorted colors

Two 14mm round fuchsia beads

Small box of straight pins

DMC embroidery needle #5

Beadalon big eye beading needle 2¼" (5.7cm)

Tapestry needle

Size G-6 (4mm) crochet hook (optional)

Techniques

Washing and felting (pages 11–12)

Appliqué (page 116)

Embroidery: Blanket stitch (page 116), running stitch (page 117), satin stitch (page 117), backstitch (page 117), lazy daisy stitch (page 117)

Crochet: Slip stitch (page 118), single crochet (page 118), chain stitch (page 118)

FELT THE SWEATER

1. Follow the general instructions for washing and felting the sweater on pages 11–12.

MAKE THE CARDIGAN

2. To turn the felted sweater into a cardigan, cut up through the front of the sweater as shown in the illustration.

cut felted sweater

3. Turn under ½" (13mm) around all edges of the sweater and the sleeves; pin if needed. Blanket stitch around all these edges, using fuchsia and beige yarns held together. Tie off the yarn; clip and weave in the ends, unless you plan to add the optional crochet trim later.

APPLIQUÉ & EMBROIDER THE FRONT

4. Trace and cut out the Button Flower template and the Double Circles, which form a round "flower." Place the Button Flower on the felt scraps and cut out three flowers, one lavender, one peach, and one gold. Place the larger circle of the round flower on the cherry-red felt and the smaller circle on red-orange felt. Cut out these circles.

5. Referring to the project photograph as a guide, pin the flowers onto the front of the jacket. For the round flower, place the red-orange circle centered on the cherry-red circle. Blanket stitch around each circle, using matching-color embroidery floss, to attach each one to the sweater front.

6. Using avocado-green yarn, the tapestry needle, and running stitch, embroider a stem from the bottom of the sweater up to each flower. Curve some of the stems. Using avocado-green yarn, the tapestry needle, and satin stitch, embroider two leaves on the stem to the round flower.

7. Sew the orange button to the center of the peach five-petal flower. As you sew it on, add four black seed beads on top of the button with an orange seed bead in the center. Repeat for the gold flower, using the red button, four lime-green seed beads, and one black seed bead. Repeat for the purple flower, using the white button, four red-orange seed beads, and one black seed bead.

APPLIQUÉ & EMBROIDER THE BACK

8. Trace and cut out the templates for the Mini Sweater and the Pants. Place the pants on the beige felt and cut them out. Place the mini sweater on the gold felt and cut it out, then place the same template on the aqua felt and cut it out.

9. Referring to the project photograph as a guide, center the three apparel motifs on the back of the sweater with the slacks in the middle. Blanket stitch around each felt piece, using matching-color embroidery floss, to attach each one to the sweater back.

folded edges under : sew

sew blanket stitch appliqué

crochet

ON THE FRONT OF THE SWEATER, THE RED-ORANGE AND
CHERRY-RED CIRCLES ARE BLANKET-STITCHED, AND THE STEM
IS CREATED WITH A RUNNING STITCH. LEAVES ARE STRAIGHT
STITCHED.

CENTER THE THREE APPAREL MOTIFS ONTO THE BACK OF THE
SWEATER, AND BLANKET STITCH EACH PIECE.

10. Embellish the gold mini sweater as follows: Using gold embroidery floss, tie a bow and sew it
to the center of the neckline. Sew on bead flowers in a diagonal row across the sweater, using
six 2mm seed beads of the same color for each flower—green, then aqua, then yellow—and
a single red-orange seed bead in the center of each flower. Using lime-green embroidery
floss and lazy daisy stitch, embroider some leaves around the three bead flowers.

11. Decorate the pants as follows: Referring to the photograph as a guide, sew a black 2mm seed
bead to the right of center of the slacks, approximately ⅜" (10mm) down from the top edge.
Sew seven orange 2mm seed beads onto the slacks, encircling the black bead. Take a beading needle and brown embroidery floss up through the top left corner of the slacks from the
inside of the sweater. Thread on nine brown 2mm seed beads. Take the needle down through
the slacks at the center left of the bead flower and back up at the center right of the bead flower.
Thread on three more brown seed beads. Take the needle to the inside of the sweater at the
upper right corner of the slacks, then knot and tie off the thread on the inside of the sweater

12. Decorate the aqua mini sweater as follows: Using aqua embroidery floss, tie a bow and sew
it to the center of the neckline. Add three bead flowers made like those on the gold mini
sweater and position them as shown in the project photograph. Use six aqua beads and one
red-orange center bead for the first flower, six red-orange beads and one yellow center bead

for the second flower, and six lime-green beads and one red-orange center bead for the third flower. Using lime-green embroidery floss and backstitch, stitch a diagonal line from the lower left corner of the shirt up to the center flower and back down to the lower right corner of the shirt. Take the needle under the beaded flowers as you stitch this line.

13. Using light-brown yarn, the tapestry needle, and running stitch, stitch a horizontal line all the way across the back of the sweater above the felt motifs.

14. Using brown embroidery floss, running stitch, and straight stitch, embroider a coat hanger in each shirt and up over the horizontal brown yarn line.

CROCHET EDGING (OPTIONAL)

15. Continue with the same two colors of yarn from the blanket stitches or attach new yarn with a slip stitch. Work a row of single crochet onto the blanket stitches from the bottom front of the sweater up and around the neckline and down to the bottom of the sweater on the other side. Turn your work. Single crochet in each single crochet for 4 more rows. Attach new fuchsia and beige yarn with a slip stitch to the bottom front corner of the sweater. Repeat the pattern, stitching around the bottom edge of the sweater (including the ends of the crocheted rows up the front of the sweater); only add 5 more rows after the first row. Repeat the same sequence around the cuffs, working continuously in rounds; add 5 more rounds after the first one. Attach new fuchsia yarn only at one upper corner of the sweater front. Single crochet in each stitch of the trim all the way around the neckline, down the front, around the bottom edge, and back up the front on the other side of the sweater. Tie off the yarn; clip and weave in the ends. Repeat single crochet with fuchsia yarn around the edges of the sleeves as well.

CROCHET TIES (OPTIONAL)

16. Attach the fuchsia yarn to one top corner of the sweater front with a slip stitch, using two strands of yarn held together as one. Chain for 14" (35.5cm). Thread the ends of the yarn through a 14mm fuchsia bead. Tie an overhand knot under the bead with both yarns still held together. Cut 3 strands of fuchsia yarn 4" (10cm) long and hold them together. Take the yarn from the tie around the center of the bunch. These, together with the yarn from the chained tie, will make a tassel. Repeat on the other side of the sweater front.

FLOWER GARDEN JACKET

This sophisticated jacket will dress up even the plainest of outfits. With the beautiful flowers on the front and the striking trim, this is sure to be one of your perennial favorites!

Finished Measurements

Neck width 6" (15.2cm)

Shoulder width 15½" (39.3cm)

Sleeve length 20½" (50.8cm)

Overall length 21" (53.3cm)

Overall width 17" (43.2cm)

Materials

Woman's forest-green sweater made of mostly feltable fibers (see pages 10–11), at least 25% larger than finished size

 1 skein each Rowan Classic Cashsoft 4-ply yarn, 57% extra fine merino, 33% microfibre, 10% cashmere, 1.75 oz (50g), 197 yd (180m), in olive green, leaf green, turquoise, mauve

Two 15mm green oval beads

Two 10mm amber beads

About 24 4mm nugget beads in assorted colors

One 20mm bone-colored oval bead for sweater closure

Three 8mm round beads in assorted colors

Small box of straight pins

DMC embroidery needle #5

Beadalon big eye beading needle 2¼" (5.7cm)

Tapestry needle

Size G-6 (4mm) crochet hook

Techniques

Washing and Felting (pages 11–12)

Appliqué (page 116)

Embroidery: Blanket stitch (page 116)
Crochet (optional): Chain stitch (page 118), single crochet (page 118), double crochet (page 119), five-petal crocheted flower (page 119)

FELT THE SWEATER

1. Follow the general instructions for washing and felting the sweater on pages 11–12.

MAKE THE JACKET

2. To turn the felted sweater into a jacket, cut up through the front of the sweater, then cut out the neck, cuffs, and bottom of the sweater. Turn all edges under ½" (13mm) and sew with a running stitch.

3. Blanket stitch across the bottom edge, the cuffs, and the neckline, using turquoise yarn and the tapestry needle. Blanket stitch down the two front edges of the sweater, using turquoise and mauve yarns held together.

CROCHET FLOWERS

4. Refer to the project photo and lay a 5" (12.5cm) length of cord vertically on each side of the sweater to create a stem. Using olive-green yarn and the tapestry needle, stitch the cords to

the sweater by working blanket stitch over them. Thread a 3" (7.5cm) double strand of olive-green yarn through the tapestry needle, and pull it from the inside of the sweater to the outside near the center of each stem to create a dangle that will simulate a tendril; vary the heights of the two dangles on the stem. Thread a green oval bead onto the yarn of each dangle and tie an overhand knot at the end of the yarn to secure each bead in place.

5. Using turquoise yarn, crochet two five-petal flowers (directions on page 119).

6. Using leaf green and olive green yarns as one, make four 2½" (6.5cm) long leaves as follows: Make a chain that is 5" (12.5cm) long. Single crochet in each chain. Turn work. Skip 2 stitches and double crochet in each stitch until you're 2 stitches from the end; tie off yarn. Fold this in half to form a leaf shape and crochet the two sides together down the center with slip stitches.

7. Sew a turquoise crocheted five-petal flower at the top of each stem. Sew two crocheted leaves, one on each side of the stem.

8. Sew an amber bead in the center of each felt or crocheted flower. Sew nugget beads around each amber bead.

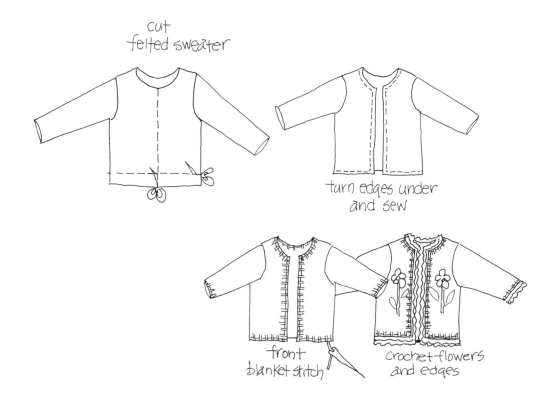

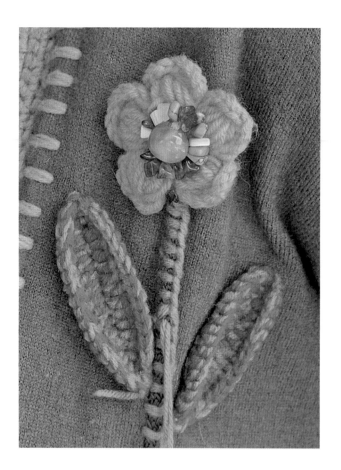

CROCHET EDGING (OPTIONAL)

9. Using turquoise and mauve yarns held together, single crochet to the blanket stitches around the edges of the sweater. Single crochet for 3 more rows around the sweater and 6 more rows around the sleeve edges. Tie off the olive-green yarn and weave in the yarn end. Continue with the turquoise yarn only and work the following ruffled crochet around the edges of the sweater and the sleeves: (Single crochet then chain 6) in each stitch around all the edges. Tie off and weave in the yarn end.

MAKE BUTTON CLOSURE

10. For closure, sew the 20mm bead to one top front corner of the sweater with the embroidery needle and green Cashsoft yarn. With turquoise and mauve yarns held together, form a loop that will fit over the bead and sew the loop to the other top front corner. If you wish, you can crochet this loop by chaining for the needed length and then working a single crochet in each chain.

FAIR ISLE FLOWERED SKIRT

Here's another unexpected use for your basic Fair Isle patterned sweater. The yoke turns into the top of the skirt, and the ribbed body becomes the bottom. The waistband is crocheted with a tie at the side. Take a big baggy Fair Isle sweater and turn it into something fun and flirty!

Finished Measurements

Small 14½" (37cm) w (at the top) x 14" (35.5cm) l, flaring out to 23" (58.5cm) w (at the bottom)

Materials

Large men's sweater, made of mostly feltable fibers (see pages 10–11), with Fair Isle pattern (use a sweater that is approximately 25% larger than your hip width)

Blanket Stitched Flower and Vein Leaf template (page 123) and tracing paper

Ready-made felt in turquoise, purple, and light green, to fit templates

1 skein each size 25 embroidery floss in turquoise, purple, and light green

SUPER FINE 1 1 skein each Rowan Classic Cashsoft 4-ply yarn, 57% extra fine merino, 33% microfibre, 10% cashmere, 1.75 oz (50g), 197 yd (180m), in olive green and tan

Two buttons, one orange and one pink, each ½" (13mm) in diameter

Ten seed beads, 5 green and 5 orange size 10/0

Small box of straight pins

DMC embroidery needle # 5

Beadalon big eye beading needle 2¼" (5.7cm)

Tapestry needle

Size G-6 (4mm) crochet hook (optional)

Techniques

Washing and felting (pages 11–12)

Appliqué (page 116)

Embroidery: Blanket stitch (page 116), running stitch (page 117), straight stitch (page 117)

Crochet (optional): Slip stitch (page 118), chain stitch (page 118), single crochet (page 118), double crochet (page 119)

To figure out the size, take your hip measurement and divide that number by half. You can adjust the length accordingly. For a size small (shown), the pieces measured 14½" wide (at the top) x 14" (37cm x 35.5cm) top to bottom, flaring out to 23" (58.5cm) wide at the bottom.

FELT THE SWEATER

1. Follow the general instructions for washing and felting the sweater on pages 11–12.

MAKE THE SKIRT

2. Following the illustration, cut two pieces that will become the skirt.

3. Place the two skirt pieces together with right sides facing. Machine-stitch or hand-sew down both sides, using a ½" (13mm) seam allowance. Leave a 1" (2.5cm) placket at the top of the left skirt seam, unless you are going to make the optional crochet band. Turn the skirt right side out. Stitch down the seam allowance in the placket area.

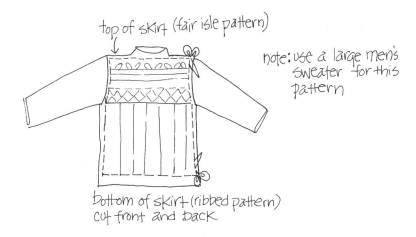

cut
felted sweater

top of skirt (fair isle pattern)

note: use a large men's
sweater for this
pattern

bottom of skirt (ribbed pattern)
cut front and back

APPLIQUÉ & EMBROIDER

4. Copy the Blanket Stitched Button Flower at 100% and 150%. Trace and cut out the Vein Leaf template. Pin the larger flower template onto the turquoise felt, the smaller flower onto the purple felt, and the leaf template onto the light-green felt. Cut out one flower of each color and two leaves.

5. Referring to the project photograph for placement, position the two flowers on the skirt front; pin the flowers in place. Blanket stitch the flowers to the skirt front, using matching-color embroidery floss. Be careful not to stitch them to the skirt back.

6. Embroider a flower stem to each flower, as shown in the project photograph, using running stitch, olive-green yarn, and the tapestry needle.

7. Position a felt leaf beside each flower stem. Blanket stitch the leaves to the skirt, using matching-color embroidery floss. Embroider veins on each leaf, using the same floss and straight stitch.

wrong side
top   sew sides
together

bottom

8. Using olive green, sew the orange button to the center of the turquoise flower. As you sew the button on, add four green seed beads on top of the button and one orange seed bead in the center of the green ones. Sew the pink button to the center of the purple flower. As you sew the button on, add four orange seed beads on top of the button and one green seed bead in the center of the orange one.

right side
blanket stitch

FINISH

9. Turn under the top and bottom edges of the skirt ½" (13mm). Blanket stitch around the bottom edge of the skirt, using olive green yarn and the tapestry needle. (If desired, you can use a crochet hook and chain 3 stitches between each vertical stitch of the blanket stitch instead of just carrying the yarn over to the next stitch.) With olive green and tan yarns, held together, blanket stitch around the top edge of the skirt.

crochet top
and tie string

Crochet bottom
(optional)

10. If you are not making the crochet band at the top of the skirt, thread onto a needle three 10" (25.5cm) lengths of olive green yarn held together to make a tie. Take the strands from the inside to the outside of the skirt at the top of one side of the placket. Remove the yarn from the needle and tie the strands together with an overhand knot. Repeat for the other side of the placket.

CROCHET BAND (OPTIONAL)

11. Using olive green and tan yarns held together, single crochet to the blanket stitch around the top edge of the skirt. Single crochet in each single crochet around the skirt for one more round. To create the placket, work four more rows back and forth as follows: On the first of these rows, skip the first single crochet, then single crochet in each stitch up to the last single crochet; skip the last single crochet; continue with single crochet back and forth for three more rows.

CROCHET TIES (OPTIONAL)

12. With olive yarn, make two 10" (25.5cm) long ties with chain stitches. Join these to the top corners of the placket with slip stitches. Tie off the yarn and weave in the yarn ends.

CROCHET TRIM (OPTIONAL)

13. Attach olive green yarn to a blanket stitch around the bottom of the skirt with a slip stitch or continue with the same yarn you were using for the blanket stitch. (Chain 5, slip stitch into the blanket stitch) all around the bottom edge for the first row. The chain stitches will form scallops around the bottom of the skirt. For the second row (chain 5, slip stitch into the center or 3rd chain of the scallop on the previous row) all around the skirt. This row is staggered with the row above. Repeat the second row 3 more times. These rows will all be staggered with the rows above. On the next row (work 5 double crochet in 1 scallop of the previous row, skip 2 scallops of the previous row) all around skirt. On the last row (single crochet in each double crochet from 1 scallop, slip stitch into the center chain of the 1st skipped scallop on the previous row, chain 10, slip stitch into the 7th chain of the chain-10 to make a circle, single crochet twice in each chain of the circle, chain 7, slip stitch into the center chain of the 2nd skipped scallop of previous row) all around skirt. Tie off the yarn and weave in the end of the yarn.

FUZZY ANGORA PULLOVER

Romance meets playfulness in this soft and fuzzy angora sweater. The crochet border on the bottom and the cuffs adds an unexpected surprise. People are going to want to pet you everywhere you go!

Finished Measurements

Neck width 6½" (16.5cm)

Shoulder width 16½" (41.9cm)

Sleeve length 24" (61cm)

Overall length 20" (50.8cm)

Overall width 17" (43.2cm)

Materials

Deep pink angora pullover sweater, made of mostly feltable fibers (see pages 10–11), three sizes too large (V-neck shown, but any style neckline will work)

Mini Heart template (page 122) and tracing paper

Scrap of previously felted sweater or ready-made felt in fuchsia to fit template

10" (25.5cm) square of cardboard

1 skein size 25 deep-pink embroidery floss

Approximately 30 clear AB sequins

Approximately 30 clear AB 2mm seed beads

 1 skein Rowan Classic Cashsoft 4-ply yarn, 57% extra fine merino, 33% microfibre, 10% cashmere, 1.75 oz (50g), 197 yd (180m), in light brown; also 1 skein fuchsia for optional crochet

Small box of straight pins

Embroidery needle #5

Beadalon big eye beading needle 2¼" (5.7cm)

Tapestry needle

Size G-6 (4mm) crochet hook (optional)

Techniques

Washing and felting (pages 11–12)

Appliqué (page 116)

Embroidery: Blanket stitch (page 116)

Crochet (optional): Slip stitch (page 118), chain stitch (page 118), single crochet (page 118), double crochet (page 119)

FELT THE SWEATER

1. Follow the general instructions for washing and felting the sweater on pages 11–12.

APPLIQUÉ & EMBROIDER

2. Trace and cut out the Mini Heart template enlarged at 350%. Pin the template onto the scrap of felted fuchsia sweater or ready-made felt and cut it out.

3. Place the square of cardboard inside the sweater so you won't sew the heart to the back of the sweater as well as the front. Referring to the project photo, pin the heart to the front of the sweater. Blanket stitch around the heart, using deep-pink embroidery floss, to attach the heart to the sweater.

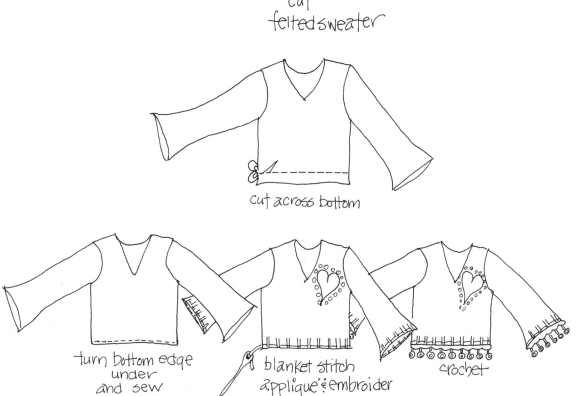

4. Using embroidery needle #5 and embroidery floss, sew an outline of sequins, with a seed bead on top of each one, all around the outside of the appliquéd heart.

FINISH

5. Cut about ½" (13mm) from the bottom edge of the sweater. Turn the hem under ½" (13mm) and sew. Blanket stitch around the bottom edge of the sweater and the cuffs, using light-brown yarn and the tapestry needle.

CROCHET TRIM (OPTIONAL)

6. With fuchsia yarn, chain 5 and join to form a circle. Double crochet three times in each chain of the circle to make a round shape. Tie off yarn and weave in the yarn end. Make approximately 54 fuchsia circles—32 for the bottom of the sweater and 11 for each sleeve.

7. The light-brown crochet trim is stitched to the horizontal areas of the blanket stitches at the bottom of the sweater with the light-brown yarn from the blanket stitching, as follows: (Chain 1 and single crochet to the first or nearest blanket stitch, work 5 double crochet into the next blanket stitch, work one single crochet and one chain into next blanket stitch. Attach the fuchsia circles as follows: Chain 7, pick up a fuchsia circle and single crochet in each fuchsia stitch around the circle to attach it to the brown trim, chain 7—the attached fuchsia circle will dangle by the chains from the trim.) Continue the sequence in parentheses around the bottom of the sweater. Tie off and weave in the yarn end. Repeat around the cuffs.

CHAPTER 4. KNITTED, FELTED & FANTASTIC:

WHEN YOU JUST HAVE TO KNIT!

This chapter is for the true knitters out there. If your hands are just itching to knit—and any knitter knows what that feels like—then these projects are for you. The patterns are very easy; even a beginning knitter can follow them. The felting and appliqué processes add yet another dimension to it. The projects listed here use fairly large-size needles and yarn, which make for very fast knitting. The yarns specified are all hand-dyed, variegated wools and wool blends (at least 85 percent wool, which is the recommended percentage for successful felting) and are highly textured. They are beautiful when knitted, and even more interesting to look at and wear after they are felted.

TRUE-BLUE KNITTED PURSE

This blue, flower-embellished purse is sweet and sassy at the same time. There is some shaping in the knitting, so you'll need to know how to decrease (knit two stitches together), but that's as complicated as it gets! The flower and grass motifs in the center and bottom are crocheted, but that part is optional. The crochet shoulder strap makes this bag a pleasure to carry around.

Finished Measurements

9" (22.9cm) w (at bottom of purse), 5½" (14cm) w at top of purse x 10" (25.4cm) h

Materials

 1 skein Fleece Artist Slubby, 100% wool, 9 oz (250g), 273½ yds (250m), color Rainforest

½ yard stiff or linen-like woven fabric for lining

Two 12mm amber beads

1 package nugget beads in assorted colors

 1 skein each Rowan Classic Cashsoft 4-ply yarn, 57% extra fine merino, 33% microfibre, 10% cashmere, 1.75 oz (50g), 197 yd (180m), in turquoise, cream, avocado green, dark green, and light brown

Off-white felted scrap 6" (15cm) round circle

Size 13 (9mm) knitting needles

Small box of straight pins

Beadalon big eye beading needle 2¼" (5.7cm)

Tapestry needle

Size G-6 (4mm) crochet needle

Techniques

Knitting (page 119)

Appliqué (page 116)

Embroidery: Blanket stitch (page 116), backstitch (page 117), lazy daisy stitch (page 117), backstitch (page 117)

Crochet: Slip stitch (page 118), single crochet (page 118), chain stitch (page 118)

KNIT THE PURSE

Front

Knit 2 pieces

1. Cast on 22 stitches. Knit in stockinette stitch (knit the first row, purl the second row, and repeat). Decrease 1 stitch at each end of every 4th row. Follow this sequence until you have 14 stitches. Knit until the piece measures 10" (25.5cm). Bind off all stitches.

Back

2. Work the same as the front.

FELT THE PURSE

3. Follow the general instructions for washing and felting the knitted pieces on pages 11–12.

4. Before embellishing and making the purse, use one of the purse pieces as a pattern and cut out two pieces of lining fabric the same size, plus ¼" (6mm), for a seam allowance on all sides.

APPLIQUÉ & EMBROIDER

5. If desired, you can substitute your favorite crochet flower pattern for the appliqué flower, making it with cream yarn and sewing on a 12mm amber bead in the center with nugget beads surrounding it.

6. Backstitch a stem under the flower using light-brown yarn. Embroider two leaves on the stem, using a lazy daisy stitch and the brown yarn. Using the beading needle and Cashsoft brown yarn, sew some nugget beads onto the flower stem.

7. Using a beading needle and avocado green Cashsoft yarn, sew about 15 nugget beads to the purse randomly below the flower.

8. If desired, crochet a long chain-stitch ruffle with avocado-green yarn, gather it up in a ruffled bunch, and sew it under the flower to simulate grass. Sew the nugget beads randomly to the crocheted grass.

ASSEMBLE THE PURSE

9. Place the front and back of the purse together, with right sides facing (embellishments will be on the inside). Using a ½" (13mm) seam allowance, sew around the sides and bottom of the purse. Trim the seam allowance to ¼" (6mm). Turn the purse right-side out.

10. Blanket stitch around the top edge of the purse, using turquoise yarn. Tie off yarn, clip, and weave in ends, unless you are adding optional crochet edging around the top.

sew front and back

wrong side facing

wash and felt

CROCHET EDGING (OPTIONAL)

11. Continuing with the yarn from the blanket stitch or attaching new yarn with a slip stitch, work two rows of single crochet around the top edge of the purse. Tie off the yarn, clip, and weave in the ends.

FINISH

12. Sew a 12mm amber button to the center top edge on the front of the purse. Sew a yarn loop to the center top edge on the back of purse large enough to slip over the bead on the front for closure. If desired, you may crochet this loop with chain stitches.

MAKE THE PURSE STRAP

13. You may braid this strap or crochet it with chain stitches. If you're braiding it, use nine strands of turquoise yarn with three strands in each group for a three-part braid. Tie all strands of yarn together with an overhand knot before braiding. Braid for 30" (76cm), then tie another overhand knot with all strands together as one. Sew the overhand knots to the inside top edge of the purse on each side. If crocheting, use four strands of yarn held together. Join to the inside top edge on one side of the purse, using a slip stitch. Chain for 30" (76cm). Join to the inside top edge on the other side of the purse. Tie off the yarn and clip the excess (the lining will cover the yarn ends).

chain stitch cord

right side

crochet ruffle

CROCHET RUFFLE (OPTIONAL)

14. Backstitch, using turquoise yarn, around the purse in the seam to create a base for the crochet ruffle. Join the new yarn at the top edge of the purse with a slip stitch, chain 6. (Single crochet to the base backstitch, but hold your needle and yarn out from the edge of the purse about ¾" [2cm] while you make the single crochet, chain 5.) Repeat the sequence in parentheses around the purse.

LINE THE PURSE

15. Pin the two pieces of lining fabric together, with right sides facing. Machine-stitch or hand-sew around the sides and bottom, leaving the top open. Do *not* turn the lining right-side out.

16. Place the lining in the purse, turn under the top edge, and whipstitch the lining to the inside top edge of the purse.

put in lining
Crochet flower & grass

COZY CELL PHONE HOLDER

This cell phone holder, which knits up in no time, is just the project for you knitters who have not yet ventured past the scarf. The piece is created in simple stockinette stitch and requires no shaping. You simply knit a rectangle, felt it, and trace your cell phone to get the right size to fit your phone. Thanks to the felting process, there is no risk of the yarn unraveling after it is cut.

Finished Measurements

To fit your cell phone

Shown 2¾" (7cm) w x 5" (12.7cm) h

Materials

5 BULKY **1 skein Yoroi yarn by Noro, 87% wool, 7% cotton, 6% silk, 3.5 oz (100g), 131 yds (120m), color #5 (burgundy tweed color)**

4 MEDIUM **1 skein Kujaku yarn by Noro, 85% wool, 15% polyester, 1.8 oz (50g), 100 yds (92m), color #23 (green and yellow color)**

Blanket Stitched Flower template (page 123) and tracing paper

Scrap of gold ready-made felt, to fit template

1 skein size 25 embroidery floss in red-violet

1 red button, ½" (13mm) in diameter

Size 10 (6mm) knitting needles

Small box of straight pins

DMC embroidery needle #5

DMC embroidery needle #18

Tapestry needle

Size G-6 (4mm) crochet hook (optional)

Techniques

Knitting (page 119)

Appliqué (page 116)

Embroidery: Blanket stitch (page 116), backstitch (page 117)

Crochet (optional): Slip stitch (page 118), single crochet (page 118)

KNIT THE PIECE

1. Using size 10 needles and Yoroi yarn, cast on 25 stitches. Knit in stockinette stitch (knit the first row, purl the second row, and repeat) until the piece measures 12" (30.5cm). Cast off all stitches.

FELT THE PIECE

2. Follow the general instructions for washing and felting the knitted piece on pages 11–12.

APPLIQUÉ & EMBROIDER

3. Trace the outline of your cell phone on a piece of paper to make a template. Lay the template on your felted knitted piece and cut out two pieces. Lay one piece on your work surface—this will be the front.

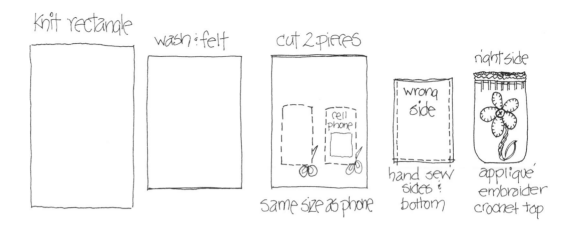

4. Trace and cut out the Blanket Stitched Flower template (page 123). Pin the template to the gold felt and cut out the flower.

5. Referring to photograph as a guide, position the flower on the front piece of the cell phone holder. Blanket stitch around the flower, using red-violet embroidery floss, to attach the flower to the knitted front of the holder. Sew the button to the center of the flower with the same embroidery floss. Embroider the flower stem, using the Kujaku yarn, the tapestry needle, and backstitch, curving it as shown in the photograph.

FINISH

6. Place the knitted front and back pieces together, with right sides facing. The flower will be on the inside. With a ¼" (6mm) seam allowance, machine- or hand-sew down both sides and across the bottom, leaving the top open. Turn the piece right-side out.

7. Blanket stitch around the top of the holder, using the Kujaku yarn and the tapestry needle. Tie off; clip and weave in the yarn end, unless you are going to add the optional crochet trim.

CROCHET TRIM (OPTIONAL)

8. Continuing with the same yarn from the blanket stitch or attaching new yarn with a slip stitch, stitch one row of single crochet to the blanket stitching around the top of the holder. Tie off; clip and weave in the yarn end.

WILD 'N' WOOLY SCARF

This wild and textured-looking scarf is made from a wool-nylon blend yarn. It is so soft to the touch that you would never believe it was wool unless you saw the label. After felting, the fiber takes on an even softer and more textured look. The appliqué heart "flowers" and embroidery on one end add a nice twist.

Finished Measurements

5¾" (14.3cm) w x 48" (121.9 cm) h

Materials

 1 skein Fleece Artist Wild 'n' Wooly, 96% wool, 4% nylon, 8.75 oz (250g), 219 yds (200m), in Rainforest

1 skein Rowan Classic Cashsoft 4-ply yarn, 57% extra fine merino, 33% microfibre, 10% cashmere, 1.75 oz (50g), 197 yd (180m), in yellow-green

Mini Heart and Double Circles templates (pages 122, 124) and tracing paper

Scraps of previously felted pieces or ready-made felt in purple, turquoise, and orange

1 skein each size 25 embroidery floss in purple, turquoise, and orange

Size 13 (9mm) knitting needles

Small box of straight pins

DMC embroidery needle #5

Tapestry needle

Techniques

Knitting (page 119)

Appliqué (page 116)

Embroidery: Blanket stitch (page 116), backstitch (page 117), lazy daisy stitch (page 117)

knit scarf

KNIT THE SCARF

1. With size 13 needles and the Wild 'n' Wooly yarn, cast on 18 stitches. Knit in stockinette stitch (knit the first row, purl the second row, and repeat) until the piece measures 60" (152.5cm). Bind off all stitches.

FELT THE PIECE

2. Follow the general instructions for washing and felting the knitted piece on pages 11-12.

wash and felt scarf

APPLIQUÉ & EMBROIDER

3. Copy the template for the Mini Heart at 150%, and trace and cut out the larger circle and the smaller circle of the Double Circles template. Pin the heart template on the orange felt, the larger circle on the purple felt, and the smaller circle on the turquoise felt. Cut out these pieces.

4. Referring to the project photograph, position the pieces on one end of the scarf. The turquoise circle is centered on the purple circle. Using matching embroidery floss, blanket stitch around each piece to attach them to the scarf.

5. Embroider a stem to each flower, using yellow-green yarn, the tapestry needle, and backstitch. Embroider a leaf on the stem to the round flower, using a lazy daisy stitch.

appliqué

TECHNIQUES — — — — — — — — — — — —

The projects throughout *Sweater Renewal* use a combination of techniques. In this guide, you will find instructions and illustrations for most of the key techniques, including appliqué, embroidery, and crochet. The projects are so simple that almost anyone can do them, whether you have mastered these techniques or not. The instructions are simple and the skill level is very easy. I hope you enjoy combining these techniques to create your own beautiful and original masterpieces!

Illustrations are provided for all appliqué, embroidery, and crochet stitches, in case you are new to the world of embellishment.

APPLIQUÉ

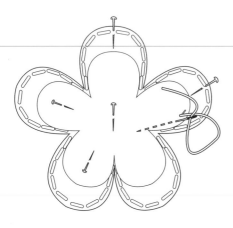

Appliqué is from the French word for "apply," and that is exactly what it is. It is a process in which smaller pieces of fabric or felt are sewn onto a larger background piece.

Appliqué pieces can be sewn on by hand or by machine. In this book, they are attached to the foundation piece with embroidery stitches, in most cases a blanket stitch done by hand.

EMBROIDERY

Embroidery refers to the embellishment of fabric using decorative stitches.

BLANKET STITCH

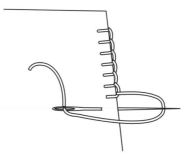

The blanket stitch was traditionally used to edge blankets. It can be worked with either yarn or embroidery floss.

Work from left to right. Secure the yarn or floss on the back of the piece (if you are edging) or on the back of the foundation piece (if you are appliquéing). With the front facing you, insert the needle a little way from the edge (depending on how large you want your blanket stitching to be, this could be from ⅛" [3mm] in from the edge on smaller pieces to ⅜" [10mm] on larger pieces). Insert the needle from the front to the back of the piece. Bring the needle to the edge of the piece and up through the loop made by the yarn or floss. Pull tight. Move to the right from ⅛" (3mm) to ⅜" (10mm), depending on the size of your blanket stitching and yarn or floss, then insert the needle again from the front to the back, away from the edge as before; bring the needle to the edge and up through the loop made by the yarn or floss; pull tight. Continue in this manner all around the piece you are edging or around the appliqué piece. Keep the spacing even between the stitches.

STRAIGHT STITCH

The straight stitch is the simplest embroidery stitch. It is just one stitch on top of the fabric. It can be a series of straight stitches to create a line or a curving line. It can also be a group of straight stitches in a radiating fashion. A **satin stitch** is a group of straight stitches side by side and close together, often used to fill in a shape.

Secure the thread on the back side. Bring the needle up to the front and over to the point you want your straight stitch to go (they can be various lengths), then back to the back side.

RUNNING STITCH

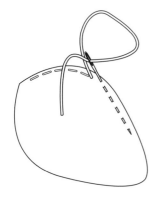

The running stitch is simply a straight or curved dashed line of straight stitches.

Secure the thread or yarn on the back side. Bring the needle up to the front, make a straight stitch of the length desired, take the needle down to the back side. Skip a small space and bring the needle back to the front. Continue in this manner to embroider a straight or curved line.

BACKSTITCH

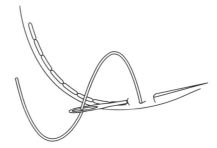

Backstitches create a solid straight or curved line.

Secure the yarn or thread on the back side. Take a small running stitch. Skip a space the length you want your stitches to be and bring the needle up to the front. Take the needle to the back through the hole at the end of your small running stitch. Skip the length of *two* stitches and bring the needle to the front; take the needle to the back through the hole at the end of your previous stitch. Repeat the the previous step for the length of the backstitch line you desire.

LAZY DAISY STITCH

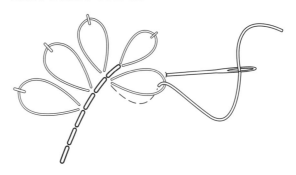

The lazy daisy stitch creates a petal shape.

Bring the needle up at the inner point of what will be the petal, and hold the thread or yarn toward you. Take the needle down to the back at the inner point of the petal just beside where you brought the needle up. Bring the needle out to the front at the outer end of the petal shape on the outside of the yarn you are holding, go over the looped thread you are holding, draw up the loop, and take the needle down directly on the other side of the looped thread or yarn.

CROSS-STITCH

Often entire designs are created with cross-stitches, or they can be used within designs created with other types of stitches. The cross-stitch comprises two diagonal straight stitches that cross each other to make an X pattern.

Make a slanting stitch from the lower left to upper right of the stitch area. Make a second slanting stitch from the lower right to the upper left that crosses the first stitch.

CHAIN STITCH

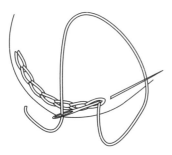

This is a decorative stitch in which loops are connected like links of a chain.

CROCHET

The word *crochet* is derived from a Middle French word that means hook. It describes the process of creating lacy-looking fabric or trims from a length of cord, yarn, or thread, using a hooked tool.

SLIP STITCH

The slip stitch is used to join work, bind off stitches, or carry yarn to a different working position without adding extra height.

Insert the hook through the loop of a previous stitch or into a slip knot from front to back. Loop the working yarn over the hook (1) and draw the hook through *both* the previous stitch *and* the original loop on the hook (2). You have made one slip stitch and have one loop remaining on the hook (3).

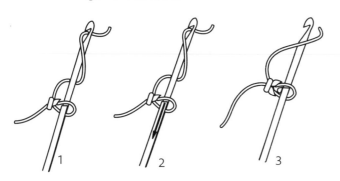

CHAIN STITCH

A length of chain stitches often forms the foundation of your crochet when there is no other foundation to be used. It can also be used as the first stitch of a row to build up to the length you need for the row. In addition, chain stitches can create spaces and join motifs.

Bring the working yarn around the hook from the back of the shaft around the front, ending at the back of the hook shaft. Draw this new yarn loop through the loop on your hook. Continue making chain stitches in the same manner until you have the length of chain you want.

SINGLE CROCHET

This stitch is the shortest in height of the four basic crochet stitches.

Insert the hook through the loop of a stitch on your foundation (previous rows, chain, or the blanket-stitch edging) from front to back. Loop the working yarn over the hook (1) and draw the hook through the stitch from the foundation *only*. You now have two loops on

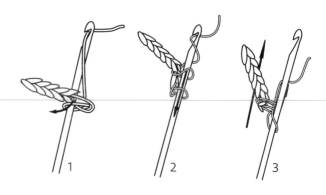

the hook (you have just made a loop in addition to the original loop on the hook). Loop the working yarn over the hook again and draw the hook through *both* loops (2). You have just made one single crochet and have one loop remaining on your hook (3). Continue your row of single crochet or other stitches the pattern calls for (4). To turn your work for subsequent rows of single crochet, chain 1 for the necessary height before beginning another row of

single crochet. The chain 1 counts as the first stitch, so skip the first stitch of the previous rows before continuing your single crochet.

DOUBLE CROCHET

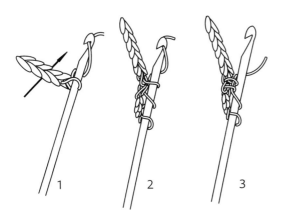

1 2 3

The double crochet is three times as high as the single crochet.

Bring the yarn over the hook from back to front (1), insert the hook in a stitch of your previous work (you now have three loops on your hook), and draw the yarn through one loop. Bring the yarn over the hook and draw it through two loops (2). Bring the yarn over the hook again and draw it through two loops (3). This completes one double crochet (4).

4

To turn your work for a subsequent row of double crochet, chain 3. The chain 3 counts as one double crochet, so begin your next row in the second stitch of the previous row.

PICOT STITCH

The picot stitch makes little loops along the edge to add a further decorative touch.

Chain 3, insert your hook into the stitch at the base of chain, bring the yarn over the hook, and draw through the loops.

FIVE-PETAL FLOWER

A crocheted flower is used on several projects in this book.

Chain 4, leaving a tail 3" to 4" (7.5–10cm) long. Join with a slip stitch to form the loop. (Chain 3, single crochet 1 into the loop) 4 times. Chain 3. Using a slip stitch, join to the base of the first chain 3. You now have five petals. Fasten off, leaving a tail 3" to 4" (7.5–10cm) long. Using the two tail ends, attach the flower to the project.

KNITTING

Knitting consists of a series of interlocking stitches that form a fabric that has "stretch" to it. Two knitting needles are required for the flat work called for in this book.

CAST ON

To cast on, make a slip knot over the left-hand needle. (Pass the right-hand needle through the loop from left to right, bring the yarn under and over the right needle, draw the yarn through the loop, and transfer the loop to the left-hand needle by inserting the left-hand needle in the loop from right to left.) Repeat the sequence in parentheses until the desired number of stitches are on the left-hand needle.

KNIT

When the desired number of stitches have been cast on, pass the right needle through the first loop on the left needle from left to right, then bring the yarn under and over the right-hand needle. Draw the yarn through and let the first stitch on the left-hand needle slip off; repeat until no stitches remain on the left-hand needle.

PURL

Bring the yarn in front of the needle, insert the right-hand needle in the first loop on the left-hand needle from right to left. Pass the yarn around the back of the right-hand needle from right to left and draw the yarn through the loop backward, letting the stitch slip off the left-hand needle. Continue to work each stitch in this manner. Be careful to have the yarn in front of you as you work.

STANDARD YARN WEIGHT SYSTEM

Yarn Weight Symbol and Category names	**1** SUPER FINE	**2** FINE	**3** LIGHT	**4** MEDIUM	**5** BULKY	**6** SUPER BULKY
Type of Yarns in Category	Sock, Fingering, Baby	Sport, Baby	DK, Light Worsted	Worsted, Afghan, Aran	Chunky, Craft, Rug	Bulky, Roving
Knit Gauge Range* in Stockinette Stitch to 4 inches	27-32 sts	23-26 sts	21-24 sts	16-20 sts	12-15 sts	6-11 sts
Recommended Needle in Metric Size Range	2.25–3.25 mm	3.25–3.75 mm	3.75–4.5 mm	4.5–5.5 mm	5.5–8 mm	8 mm and larger
Recommended Needle in U.S. Size Range	1-3	3-5	5-7	7-9	9-11	11 and larger
Crochet Gauge* Ranges in Single Crochet to 4 Inches	21-32 sts	16-20 sts	12-17 sts	11-14 sts	8-11 sts	5-9 sts
Recommended Hook in Metric Size Range	2.25–3.25 mm	3.5–4.4 mm	4.5–5.5 mm	5.5–6.5 mm	6.5–9 mm	9 mm and larger
Recommended Hook in U.S. Size Range	B-1 to E-4	E-4 to 7	7 to I-9	I-9 to K-10 ½	K-10 ½ to M-13	M-13 and larger

* GUIDELINES ONLY: The above reflects the most commonly used gauges and needle or hook sizes for specific yarn categories.

Sweaters

Most of the projects in *Sweater Renewal* were made with sweaters found at thrift shops and vintage clothing stores in my local area. Others came from closets—mine and anyone else's that I was able to rummage through. Your own closet is a great place to start, but you may also want to try garage sales and flea markets. Once you become aware of all the woollen treasures that are just waiting to be discovered, you will always be on the lookout. And part of the fun, after all, is the hunt!

Suppliers

With the exception of the sweaters, all the materials used to complete the projects in the book are readily available at your local yarn and craft stores. The companies listed below are the manufacturers of the materials I used in the book. All the websites have store locators so you can find products near you.

Yarn

Fleece Artist Yarns
www.fleeceartist.com
E-mail: sales@fleecertist.com

Noro Yarns
www.knittingfever.com
E-mail: knittingfever@knittingfever.com

Rowan Classic Yarns
www.rowanyarns.co.uk

DMC Yarns
www.dmc.com

Ready-Made Wool Felt

La Lana Wools
www.lalanawools.com
505-758-9631 (info)
888-377-9631 (orders)

Beads, Sequins, Bells, and Other Adornments

Michaels
www.michaels.com

Wooden Purse Handles

Sunbelt Fasteners
www.sunbeltfastener.com
Email: info@sunbeltfastener.com

TEMPLATES

The following templates will need to be photocopied before you pin them to your felted sweater. Some will need to be enlarged on the copier; see the pattern instructions for enlargement specifications. In small quantities, for personal use, you are free to make photocopies from this book.

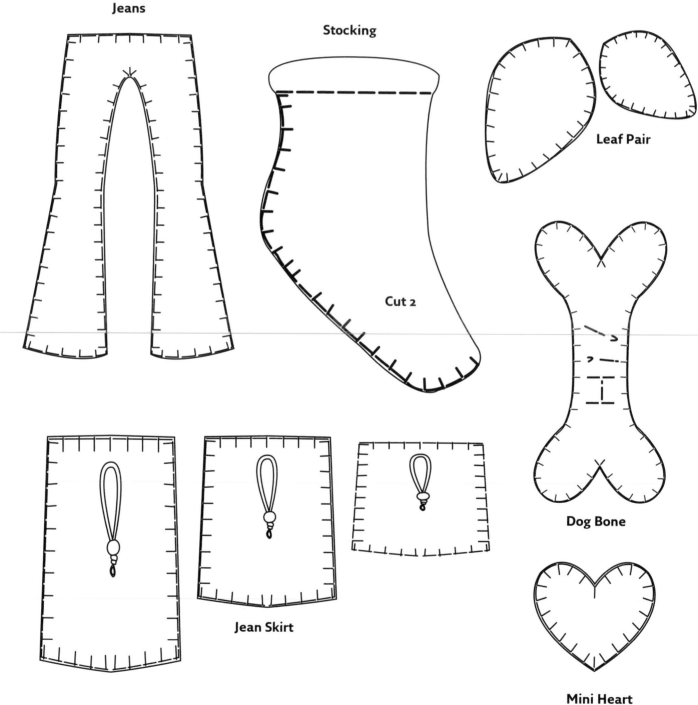

Jeans

Stocking

Cut 2

Leaf Pair

Dog Bone

Jean Skirt

Mini Heart

Double Flower

Oversized Heart

Double Hearts

Vein Leaf

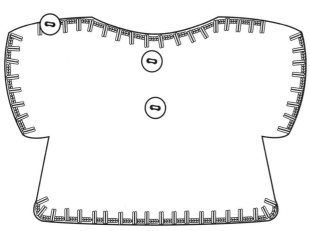

Wooly Bear Sweater

Blanket Stitched Flower

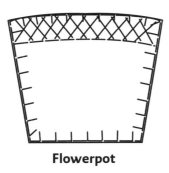

Flowerpot

Button Flower

Winged Hearts

Wooly Bear

Straight Stitched Heart

Double Circles

Heart Sweater

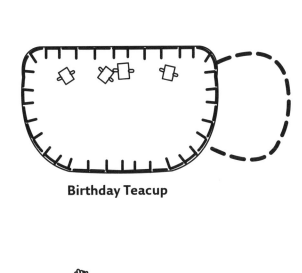

Birthday Teacup

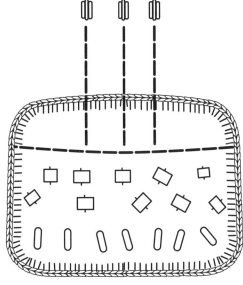

Birthday Cake

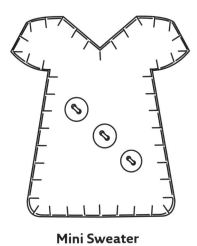

Birthday Purse

Birthday Heart

Half Flower

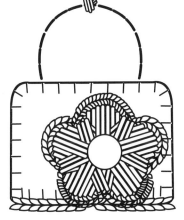

Mini Sweater

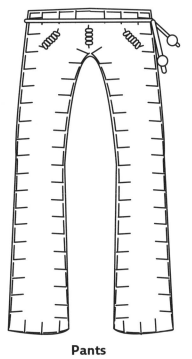

Pants

ACKNOWLEDGMENTS

Writing this book has been a labor of love, and a "first" for me in many ways. It would have been an overwhelming endeavor without the help and expertise of many amazing and talented people. My love and thanks go out to you all.

To Rosy Ngo—you have incredible insight and vision. I am so grateful that our paths crossed and that I was lucky enough for my work to catch your eye.

To Christina Schoen, my editor at Potter Craft—thank you for your patience, input, expertise, and understanding. You made this whole process a lot less intimidating than it could have been for a first-time author.

To Mordechai Alvow, stylist extraordinaire and a very dear friend—you worked your magic (as always). You bring an incredible talent and energy to everything you touch.

To all my models—everyone did such an amazing job in their own way. Ilana—your poise, stamina, and beauty go far beyond your seven years of age. Betsy—your red hair caught my eye, and the camera's as well. Anitra, you tall, blond Texan—talk about being in the right place at the right time. The luck was all mine. Elizabeth—your dark eyes, dark hair, and cuteness shine through in every photograph. Ariane— you make it all look so easy and natural. Baby Clark—your good nature and beautiful dark eyes made it so effortless. Jake and Luke, the two English springer spaniels—you give the phrase "will work for food" a whole new meaning!

To Sylvia Carroll—your expert technical editing was a lifesaver. Thanks for all your hard work and the fast turnaround. To Janine LeCour—your talent, along with your eagerness and flexibility, make you a true professional.

To Christine and Owen, the husband-and-wife team that make up Anthony-Masterson Photographers—you two were such a delight and pleasure to work with. I can't wait to do it again! You both really were incredible, and your photography speaks for itself.

To all my friends, family, and believers out there—there are too many of you to name, and not enough words to express my gratitude, but you all know who you are and how important you are in my life.

To all my employees and customers at Two Stix, my retail store in Atlanta—you all make my "own little world" a great place to be. To Beth Casner, my favorite employee (and musician), you know I couldn't do it all without you.

To my amazing daughter, Amanda—your innate sweetness, radiant energy, and incredible artistic talent continue to awe and inspire me on a daily basis. You have been my very own "in-house" editor (quite literally). Watching you grow up has been one of the highlights of my life, and being able to write this book and have you around for the process has been another.

INDEX

Page numbers in *italics* indicate illustrations.